OPEN THE TELEPATHIC CHANNEL TO YOUR PET—
with advice from Animal Planet's resident pet psychic
Sonya Fitzpatrick.

MEET SONYA'S SUCCESS STORIES:

AMADEUS: a dog whose aggressive behavior almost got him
kicked off his flyball team—until Sonya uncovered his painful past.

LINCOLN: a beautiful bird who confided to Sonya that he shredded his favorite pillow as a way of letting his owner know that he
missed her.

MR. CLINKER: a cat whose painful tumor disappeared under
Sonya's healing touch.

JEAN LaFITTE: a turtle whose unsuitable habitat lead to an
almost fatal loss of appetite—until a long chat with Sonya turned
his life around.

SONYA FITZPATRICK
THE PET PSYCHIC

What the Animals Tell Me

BERKLEY BOOKS, NEW YORK

B

A Berkley Book
Published by The Berkley Publishing Group
A division of Penguin Group (USA) Inc.
375 Hudson Street
New York, New York 10014

Animal Planet and the Animal Planet logo are registered trademarks of
Discovery Communications, Inc., used under license.

PRINTING HISTORY
Berkley hardcover edition / March 2003
Berkley trade paperback edition / March 2004

Berkley trade paperback ISBN: 0-425-19414-0

The Library of Congress has catalogued the Berkley hardcover edition as follows:

Fitzpatrick, Sonya, 1940–
Sonya Fitzpatrick, the pet psychic : what the animals tell me / Sonya
Fitzpatrick.—1st ed.
p. cm.
New York : Berkley Books, 2003.
ISBN 0-425-19290-3
1. Fitzpatrick, Sonya, 1940–. 2. Animal communicators—Texas—Houston—
Biography. 3. Pet psychics—Texas—Houston—Biography. 3. Human-animal
communication—Anecdotes. 4. Telepathy—Anecdotes. I. Title.

SF411.45.F58 A3 2003
133.8'2—dc 21   2002043865

PRINTED IN THE UNITED STATES OF AMERICA

10 9 8 7 6 5 4 3 2 1

To my beloved Rhodesian Ridgeback, Bella, for the joy and happiness she brought to our family over so many years and for her steadfast loyalty and devotion

Photo © 1996 by Patricia B. Smith

CONTENTS

PREFACE

*I*t's hard to believe that it has been seven years since my story was first told. Many things have happened since that time. I have learned much more from my animal friends. I now have my own weekly national television show, *The Pet Psychic*, on Animal Planet, and many other wonderful opportunities are on the horizon. The success of my books, seminars and television show have given me a platform that will allow me to help animals even more.

Animals have taught me everything I know. By stepping into their world, I have been able to understand their emotions, their divine intelligence and how much more they understand and are in tune with our universe than we humans. They feel impending atmospheric and geological changes in the earth in their physical bodies because they are much more in tune with all the physical elements of our earth—its electrical and magnetic fields—than we humans are. That's how their language travels. That is also how they sense things that we cannot. By sensing and feeling the earth's magnetic fields, birds intuitively fly straight and true to their winter homes thousands of miles away. Migrating whales do the same thing.

I feel privileged that so many animals have allowed me to enter their world. They have taught me their language and shared their incredible experiences with me. I feel very humbled that they have trusted me. Many people tell me they too have shared communication with their own animal friends. They are now beginning to understand that animals do have a silent language that is truly a wonder of nature.

My experiences over the last few years have taken me to an even deeper level of understanding of our animal companions. They trust me because they know I care about them and love them with a passion. When you truly feel that deep love and compassion for the animals that share your life, then you will receive a precious gift in return—their love and trust.

INTRODUCTION

*H*ow often does one hear from devoted animal lovers, "I wish there was some way I could know what my pet is thinking and feeling." Well, there is such a way, but most people do not understand that they can connect their own human mind energy to their animal's mind energy and communicate. They believe what many of us have been told from early childhood: It's impossible to communicate with our pets on any meaningful level. People don't realize that there is something unseen that exists between humans and animals—a telepathic channel we can all access to communicate with the animals we love.

I was fortunate as a child to be fully tuned in to this channel. Talking to animals was as natural for me as breathing. In fact, because of a profound hearing loss in both my ears that doctors did not discover until I was almost eleven, it was actually easier for me to understand what animals were communicating to me telepathically than what humans were communicating to me verbally. It was only as I grew older that I began to realize not everyone could "talk" to animals in this same way.

As I'll explain in chapter 1, at the age of ten, a heartbreaking trauma made me cut off the telepathic communication I had always enjoyed with my animal friends. Many years passed, and I was an adult when I rediscovered the ability to speak telepathically with animals. Then in the spring of 1994, I experienced an angelic visitation that was to change my life. Shortly thereafter, St. Francis himself, the patron saint of animals, visited me to tell me he wanted me to help him work with animals.

Soon, I felt the door to the world of communication with our animal friends opening once again. At first, it was a bit confusing for me, and difficult to understand that I had been chosen for this work. But as the weeks passed, I felt my awareness of animal communication steadily increasing. My lifelong love for animals had culminated in this special gift.

I now know I have been chosen to help animals, to educate people about the often cruel or thoughtless ways that animals are treated, and to enlighten them about what they can do to make life easier for their pets. I do this by talking to animals and finding out how they think and feel.

People often ask me how I "talk" to animals, how I make myself understood, and how I manage to understand what they are saying back to me. The method I use, though perhaps not widely known, is neither complex nor mystical. I use my mind's energy, sometimes called telepathy, to communicate with animals, to discover what is worrying them, what they like or dislike, and what makes them happy.

If they are hurting or hungry, I feel those sensations in my own body. A pleasantly full sensation tells me the animal is being regularly fed, while gnawing hunger pangs tell me just the opposite. If the animal has an ear or bladder infection, or is stiff with arthritis, I feel the exact symptoms in the correlating parts of my own body.

Every living thing—plants, trees, animals, humans—gives off energy, and it is this energy I tune in to with my mind to establish communication with animals. It is easier to communicate in this way with animals than with other humans because animals are receptive to telepathic transmissions, whereas most humans, through years of conditioning, are not.

Telepathic communication is a universal language that transcends boundaries of time, distance and species. Many people unwittingly use telepathic communication when they have come to know their animal very well. They may think of it as reading the animal's body language, but whatever they call it, telepathy is a higher form of communication, which uses a completely different part of our brain than what we use in our day-to-day lives; a part most of us rarely access. Humans know simply that their dog or cat responds to their spoken commands or whistles, never realizing they may be communicating with their pets on this higher telepathic plane.

Though animals communicate quite readily telepathically, humans have to learn to relax enough to be receptive to this form of communication. With a bit of concentration, each of us are capable of connecting on the telepathic level with an animal we love. We can learn to exchange mind energy with our pets, transmitting pictures and information back and forth with astounding speed, as there is no time or space as we understand them on the telepathic level.

Humans rely on speaking for communication because that is what is easiest and most natural for us, so we tend to discount the notion there might be an alternative way to convey thoughts, ideas, information, emotions and feelings. But just because animals do not speak with words as humans do does not mean they do not communicate. Animals communicate with pictures and feelings they transmit telepathically. You may not realize it, but we humans can and do communicate telepathically in that same way. Let me give you an example.

If I asked you to tell me, "Where is the Statue of Liberty?" your first impression would be a picture in your mind. Your thoughts would create a detailed mental image of the statue and its environs almost instantaneously. In your mind (or imagination), you would be able to "see" the torch held high in one hand, the spikes of Liberty's crown, and the surrounding water. At the same moment you were "seeing" these things, you might feel a sense of amazement, or wonder how they built such a large statue.

You probably think this picture and these thoughts and feelings exist only in your imagination, but in fact at the moment you imagine it, that same picture you see so clearly in your mind begins transmitting out telepathically from your energy. If your dog or cat is nearby, they will receive the picture and perhaps start wondering why you are thinking of a large statue. If you look at them now, you might even catch the look of puzzlement on their faces.

We regularly lay out our plans in our heads before we do anything. We dream, we think great thoughts, we hatch ideas, we play out scenes. All this mental activity is broadcast telepathically as we produce it. These pictures, plus the feelings and emotions that accompany them, are the basic building blocks of telepathic communication, just as words are the building blocks of spoken communication.

Many people are not aware they have the ability to communicate in another language because they believe that spoken language is sufficient to cover all their communication needs. But this other, telepathic language is the language animals understand, and if you can master it, even on a very elementary level, you will greatly increase your understanding of your pet's motivations, which in turn will lead to a closer and more satisfying relationship with your pet.

You are probably not consciously aware of creating pictures from your mind energy or thoughts, even though you may see them in your mind or imagination while you are creating them. As soon as you see the picture and verbally relate or explain whatever thoughts that accompany that picture, your mind races on to its next task and transfers the picture you have just created into the storage area of your brain known as short-term memory.

But the picture does not die there. Your animal sees these pictures you send out, and picks up not only all the pictures, but also the feelings, emotions, and ideas that accompany the picture as they go out telepathically from your mind through your physical body. You are constantly creating such pictures each time you think of something, and transmitting thoughts and emotions as you react to various stimuli during the course of your day. Though animals do learn the rudiments of human speech from living with us and react reliably to certain key words, it is the telepathic pictures, thoughts and emotions you send out that your animals use to make sense of you and the human world.

All animals speak this universal language, even species such as birds, turtles, and fish. When I hear an "expert" declaring certain animals to be dumb, it makes me sad, because I know from firsthand conversations with many different species how intelligent animals are. Often, as you will discover in this book, their stories are quite entertaining.

Not enough has been written about animal sensitivity, their intuition and intelligence, and the love and care they show to each other and to their humans. Pets are very much like humans in their feelings and emotions, which makes them very sensitive to human emotions. They understand all the problems within their home. If the owner is depressed, they feel the unhappiness. If the owner is happy, they feel the same way.

This is not to anthropomorphize animals, but rather to finally acknowledge that they do experience emotions not too dissimilar from our own. Animals are certainly well aware of their own feelings, and pet owners and people who work closely with animals are quick to tell you their animal companions display behavior that is difficult not to interpret as emotional. We've all seen dogs smiling and heard cats sighing with contentment.

Yet, until recently, the world of feelings was considered exclusively a human province. Fortunately, that is changing. Even scientists are now beginning to accept that animals do experience emotion, though they may be loath to attach that particular word to their observations. In their wonderful book, *When Elephants Weep*, Jeffrey Masson and Susan McCarthy make a convincing argument for the rich and complex emotional lives they have observed among animals in the wild.

But animals experience far more than simple emotion and far more than we give them credit for. They have incredible memories. They never forget when they have been hurt, and they never forget a kindness. If there is a change in their behavior, I have come to understand there is always a very good reason for that change and that the reason, which may seem inexplicable to their humans, makes perfect sense when viewed from the animal's perspective. In fact, upon investigation, I often find the problem originates with the owner, not the animal.

If we as pet owners and animal lovers are sensitive and observant, then we, too, can understand our pets and their behavior in new and rewarding ways. It is not difficult to do, though each of you will achieve varying degrees of success depending upon your openness to telepathic communication, your persistence, the relationship you have with your animal to begin with, and the animal's willingness to communicate telepathically and proficiency in doing so.

At the end of this book, I will explain how you may achieve a higher level of communication with the animals in your care. But first, I will tell you a little about my background, and how I came to this work of animal communication. Then I will share some of the wonderful stories of pets and their owners who have been helped by St. Francis and my angel guides—some healed of an illness, some restored to their rightful homes after being lost, others simply guided into more desirable behavior. Hopefully these stories will offer you insight into what your pets are thinking.

Whether or not you believe I can truly "talk" to animals is unimportant. What matters is that you treat your pets with the greatest love, kindness and courtesy possible. With patience, sensitivity, awareness, and the conscientious application of the principles I have employed in my relationships with members of the animal kingdom, principles which are outlined in this book, it is possible for many animal lovers to establish telepathic communication with their pets. If the stories in this book open the way for you to enhance and develop further the loving relationships you enjoy with your pets, I will have achieved my purpose.

St. Francis has asked me to help animals, and I pass that request along to you. All that our pets want is love and security. It is my wish that after you read this book, you will have some insight into the importance of demonstrating that love to your pet on a daily basis.

CHAPTER ONE

Little Pigs Have Big Ears

My Early Life

When I was a child in England, I spent many happy hours talking to the animals in my village. It was not the imaginary talk so many children use; I actually communicated with animals and held daily conversations and consultations with my favorites. I found out their likes and dislikes, how they felt about each other, and what made them sad and happy.

In the typically egocentric way of a child, I thought everyone could talk to animals the same way I did. I had no idea as yet that I was different in that respect, and that to other people the idea of actually communicating with animals in any sort of intelligible way was completely unthinkable. So when I told my family I talked to animals, they thought I was simply being very imaginative.

I lived with my parents, Russell and Cora Smith, my sisters, Dawn and Coral, and brother, Gordon, in Hartwell, Northhamptonshire, in the Midlands section of England. My father was a businessman in the village. He had a grocery and several other business concerns. There, I was known as "Sunny" because of my outgoing disposition and golden-blond hair.

I was the third child, and spent a great deal of time with my maternal grandmother, Emmaline Robishaw, because my mother was busy working and had little appreciation for what she called my "vivid imagination." I used to try to impress my mother by saying, "I've been on my best behavior, Mummy," to which she'd reply, "You haven't got any best behavior, Sunny."

My grandmother Robishaw was a very beautiful woman and I adored her. Her cottage was beautifully kept and provided me with a cozy retreat from the rigors of my family life. We often sat together during the long winter evenings, while she taught me to sew, knit and read, hobbies which I enjoy to this day. I loved to operate her old treadle machine. I used my feet to push the platform back and forth, leaving my hands free to guide the fabric through the needle.

I had my own bedroom at my grandmother's cottage and lived mostly there, rather than with my family. Grandmother's cottage was very close to my parents' home, so it was easy for me to go back and forth as necessary.

Grandmother gave me my own little corner of her cottage garden so I could plant flowers from seeds. She taught me how to put the seeds in the ground just so; then each day I would go with my little watering can and gently water them. My favorite time was when my hard work was rewarded with a garden full of fragrant, lovely blossoms.

Grandmother's cottage garden was spectacular, full of heirloom roses, lilacs, and lots of other beautiful flowers. We spent many happy hours in her garden. That is where I first encountered frogs. Grandmother taught me how essential frogs were to the life of a garden because they ate all the insects.

She also taught me how clever the bees were. She used to

tell me, "See how the bees kiss the flowers?" She told me they did that to get the pollen, which they then took back to their hive to make honey. I marveled at how hard the bees worked to make honey, which I loved to eat.

Watching bees was just one of our pastimes. Grandmother taught me I must always honor all creatures, no matter how insignificant they might seem to me. She said each one had its place in God's universe, and that if I was observant, I could begin to understand what that place was and how all animals worked together for the good of nature.

On summer evenings, the two of us would go for walks through Salcey Forest. When we happened upon a particularly beautiful spot, we would put down a blanket and sit very quietly, not moving or making a sound. Those times were very special to me. We saw many beautiful forest creatures as we sat there: a shy and gentle family of deer; rabbits hopping across the clearing; red squirrels; and bushy-tailed foxes. She understood that I could talk to animals in a way no other child of the village could and made sure I had the opportunity to observe wild creatures in their natural habitats. Those times in Salcey Forest were wonderful for us both, and when I look back and remember today, it still brings me a feeling of happiness.

BACK then, I had a small terrier named Judy, my first dog. She would always tell me if she felt cold. English winters can be very bitter, and we often had snow. Animals do feel the cold, especially when there are drastic changes in temperature. When I told my parents that Judy was cold, Father said she had a fur coat to keep her warm enough. But I knew my father was wrong about that, because when Judy transmitted her body temperature to me, I felt cold in my own body.

When Judy was cold, I would get one of my baby sister Coral's woolen knitted jackets and put it on her. Then I would lay her on the sofa and cover her with a blanket. She laid on her back with her little paws over the top of the blanket, telling me she felt very happy when she was warm, and very unhappy when she was cold.

I knew the blue-and-white striped jacket was Judy's favorite coat because she telepathically transmitted a picture to me of the jacket. My family was amazed that the dog allowed me to do the things I did for her, because she could and did nip if someone tried to do something she did not like. But Judy always had a wonderful temperament around me, and we loved each other dearly. The difference with me was that I spoke to her telepathically, so I knew her likes and dislikes. I often told my mother that if people would listen to Judy, they would know what she wanted.

Some people are very active and talk with their hands, but Judy did not like people running about or moving their arms very quickly. It startled her and made her feel uncomfortable, so she nipped to let people know she did not like it. Nor did she like bicycles going very fast. She said it made her feel dizzy, so she chased them. I was careful to always move very slowly when I was with Judy to keep from alarming her.

When Judy was approaching the end of her life, I told her death was nothing to fear. I told Judy that when she died, she was going to heaven where God lived. My grandmother had told me God had a beautiful garden and lots of fields for the animals to play in. I told Judy that one day I would meet up with her and play with her in God's heavenly fields, and she would never be cold again.

As Judy grew older, I realized I could feel in my own body the aches and pains the old dog was experiencing. I learned how to soothe those aches by laying my small hands upon her body. I didn't truly understand what I was doing; I just knew I could do it. I also began to understand why she was often grumpy and cross with people. I envied her the option she had of simply nipping at people who annoyed her; it was something I frequently wished I could do. But I acted out my frustrations over my parents' indifference in the time-honored fashion of any child who feels she has been neglected or misunderstood.

I did outrageous things, like putting our chickens over the fence into the neighbor's garden. Mr. Breyfield was always complaining about my cats going into his garden, but that was nothing compared to the damage our chickens could do. I told the incredulous birds they could eat all Mr. Breyfield's green vegetables and the all-too-willing accomplices didn't stop until their tummies were ready to burst. I was never found out. When asked, I told my father the gate between our two yards must have been left open by accident. This was just one of my many adventures with my animal friends.

I soon became aware I could tune in to how any animal was feeling simply by concentrating. The baker, Mr. Sturgess, went through the village with a horse-drawn cart delivering fresh bread. People would come out of their houses and shops to get a loaf and exchange a bit of gossip. When the baker's horse, Pickles, stopped outside my father's shop, I closed my eyes and my leg started aching. That's how I knew the old workhorse's leg was hurting too. Soon, I realized Pickles was telling me about his sore leg, and asking for my help to feel better.

When I ran my hands gently over Pickle's face and asked him if he would allow me to help him with his pain, he always said yes. Because I was not yet tall enough to reach up to him, Pickles lowered his head for me so I could stroke him. I put my hands on his poor leg and stroked it, all the while telling him it would be better. I felt a sensation of heat in my hands while I was doing this, and felt what I now know was healing energy flowing through me to the horse. Finally, the baker climbed back into his wagon, but not before the old horse thanked me for removing the soreness from his leg. Even the baker seemed to understand that I had some sort of beneficial effect on Pickles, who could then complete his rounds in comfort, free from the pain and stiffness in his old arthritic foreleg. That was the beginning of my phenomenal gift for healing animals.

I loved the great old workhorse. Sometimes, Pickles asked me to go with them to complete their rounds. He said I could ride on his back. So I would ask Mr. Sturgess to lift me up and I would ride the rest of the way perched high upon the noble steed, feeling like a princess.

I liked to visit the old horse in his field when he wasn't at work pulling the baker's cart. I brought him apples and carrots, and we passed many a pleasant hour chatting amicably. Pickles grumbled because he had worked hard all his life, and did not want to go on working indefinitely. But he feared Mr. Sturgess could not manage without him.

Though Mr. Sturgess was a kindly man who treated Pickles with affection and respect, he was greatly dependent on the old horse. Pickles knew the baker's route by heart. He knew where Mr. Sturgess had to go into a home to take bread to an invalid, and where people would come out to chat. Mr. Sturgess feared he could never find another horse as well-suited to the work as Pickles.

After the baker's rounds were completed, Mr. Sturgess drove to the pub, where, like most men of the village, he enjoyed spending a couple of hours each day discussing news and downing a few pints of ale. Pickles dropped him off at the Rose and Crown, then pulled the empty wagon back home by himself. Once there, he pawed the ground outside the cottage door until Mrs. Sturgess came to unharness him from the baker's cart and release him into the field. He did this every day except Sunday, which was his day off.

Mrs. Sturgess really loved Pickles, and he loved her in return. She also treated the old horse with great kindness and love, stroking him as she unfastened his harness. She knew Pickles had arthritis, so she soothed him by telling him she had a lot of pain in her bones too. "I know your poor old bones hurt like mine, duck," she told him affectionately.

Pickles was something of a sensation in our village. We all considered him a very smart horse for figuring out how to get himself home, and not waiting outside the pub in all sorts of weather for Mr. Sturgess to finish his pint. When Mr. Sturgess pulled up outside the Rose and Crown and tied the reins over the horse's head so that he would not catch them in his legs as he walked home, Pickles knew he was through for the day. "Pickles, go and have your rest," Mr. Sturgess would say. We all knew the baker would stagger home a couple of hours later after having a few pints of beer.

Sometimes I was in the village and Pickles asked me to walk back home with him, which I always did. When the apple trees were bearing in the fall, he liked to walk past Miss Bilton's, the schoolteacher's house, and help himself to a couple of choice apples. She didn't mind sharing as we were all fond of the horse. When he couldn't get over to Miss Bilton's, he often asked me to bring him apples in the field. Many times in the middle of a school day, Pickles telepathically sent me a picture of a rosy apple, and I knew he wanted me to bring him one after school. He liked ripe apples much more than green ones.

* * *

PICKLES was great friends with Blackey, a lovely black pony who belonged to Derek, my brother Gordon's friend. Like Pickles, Blackey was also a working horse. He delivered milk from Derek's dairy farm to the lorry, which then took it to the factory where it was bottled.

Folly Farm was about three miles from the village. Derek had taken it over after the death of his father. I spent many an idyllic afternoon ambling along the road to the dairy, picking poppies, buttercups, and daisies, and talking with my animal friends along the way. I knew all the cows by name as English farmers in those days had the habit of naming each of their milk cows. I made up names for the sheep and called out to them as they grazed in the lush fields and pastures adjoining the road. Sometimes, so many cows and sheep followed me along the road and through the fields that it looked like I was leading a herd.

Derek's wife, Hill, did most of the actual physical labor on the farm. She milked the dairy herd twice a day while her husband went fishing. The cows all walked up to the top of the hill when it was milking time. When the milking was done, Hill loaded the milk cans into the cart, and Blackey pulled the cart up to the factory. After Blackey's work was done, Hill turned him out into the field to graze and relax a bit. On some days when I asked for a ride, Blackey said yes, but on others, he said no, and no matter how I tried to convince him, he wouldn't be caught. He'd run full speed in the opposite direction, tossing his shiny black mane and tail as if to say, "Not today! You can't have a ride today!" But on those days when he did allow me to ride, Blackey took great care of me. He would not buck or run too fast.

When we rambled along the country lanes together, Blackey

often stopped to nibble on grass. I liked to get off his back and point out particularly succulent patches, calling out, "Look Blackey! There's some juicy grass over there!" Then I would sit at his feet while he ate.

Sometimes I harnessed Blackey to his trap and went to my father's shop in the village to get groceries for Hill. I always made sure to get a big, juicy apple for Blackey.

Blackey loved to visit Pickles as much as I did. The two were great friends. I used to tell them how important they were because they worked so hard and were so vital to the commerce of the village.

THERE was another horse in the field next to Pickles, a very beautiful horse named Star. All she had to do was take Mr. Smart's daughter, Sue, for the occasional ride. Both Blackey and Pickles thought Star was very cosseted and spoiled, but they liked her nonetheless and admired her great beauty.

All three horses were frightened of the village blacksmith, whom they said was not very kind to them. Blackey and Pickles told me they had heard him saying that horses were stupid, and that I was stupid as well for all the fantastic stories I made up about being able to talk to animals.

Blackey and Pickles told me what happened to old Mrs. Bobbitt's horse, Rosy, after she died. Mrs. Bobbitt had placed the animal in the blacksmith's care, and asked him to make sure her beloved horse went to a good home. Instead, he had sold Rosy to the slaughterhouse for meat. Blackey and Pickles begged me to convince their respective owners not to leave them in the blacksmith's care should they pass on, and so I did.

The blacksmith regularly went into my father's store to buy a meat pie for his noon meal. One day he came in and ordered his usual and I called out, "Let me get it for you, Dad." My father was more than happy to let me assist him, as he liked to exchange news and gossip with his customers, and the blacksmith was no exception.

I never could understand how the blacksmith could talk about other people when he himself was the talk of the village, always visiting Mrs. Biggles whenever her husband was away from home. I often overheard people telling my father, "There he is at Mrs. Biggles's again, and she with her curtains drawn for hours. I think it's disgusting!" When I asked my dad what was disgusting with Mrs. Biggles and the blacksmith, he just replied, "Little pigs have big ears!"

On this particular day I decided to punish the blacksmith for his unkindness to Pickles and Blackey, and for what he did to Rosy. Before I gave him his pie, I smothered it in a cloud of black pepper, then wrapped it in grease-proof paper and handed it to him with a big smile. Then I slipped off to the back room where I could watch as he took his first bite. The blacksmith started to choke and his face turned bright red. At that point I made a hasty exit out the back door of my father's shop and stayed away for a reasonable length of time, at least until I stopped laughing.

When I arrived back home in time for tea, Father said he wanted to see me. He asked me if I had put the pepper in the blacksmith's meat pie. He had found the pepper pot in the shop to be almost empty and the day before it had been almost full. I told him no, that it must have been an accident at the factory. My father was very angry and told me I had to stack shelves in the store for the next week. I hated stacking shelves but it was worth the punishment just to see the satisfaction on the faces of Pickles and Blackey when I told them the story. I decided that from that point on if I could find any way to annoy the black-smith, I would.

OUR vicar's cottage sat just within the embrace of Salcey Forest. The Reverend Canon Vandeleur Martin made his home there, along with his cheerful wife and two amazing animals, Bertie, a small Jack Russell terrier, and Jeremiah, a highly intelligent cat who sat daily just inside the vestibule of the vicarage. From this perch, he watched the world go by. Bertie and Jeremiah were great friends and each looked after the other.

Each day, Jeremiah and Bertie accompanied Mrs. Martin when she came to my father's shop. She was a petite, dark-haired woman who walked with a limp because one of her legs was shorter than the other. This affliction puzzled me greatly; I couldn't understand how this could be. When I finally gathered my courage to ask her, she smiled and told me she had been born that way. It didn't bother her at all; in fact, she considered it a blessing.

On occasion I met with Mrs. Martin as I was returning from a visit at my grandmother's cottage. I always looked forward to walking with her and her two animal companions. Jeremiah had decided he would rather be a dog and was determined that the next time he returned to earth in physical form it would be as a dog. He asked me if I was happy being a human or would I rather be an animal. I considered my life and told him yes, that although I thought animals much nicer than humans, on the whole I was quite happy and content to be a human girl.

My father had two assistants at his shop—Pat and Aunt Rene. Pat always seemed cross to me. She walked stiffly as if she were suffering from rheumatism. Her chief pride in life was her knitting and she frequently mentioned the knitting prize she had won at the Women's Institute Craft Fair. Aunt Rene was so called because she was the village mortician, and she told me that after you had washed a family's naked relative and prepared them for burial, they thought of you as family too so everyone called her "Aunt." Aunt Rene was famous for always wearing a blue knitted beret, and also for the fact that she carried her beloved stuffed cat, Tiger, about the house with her as she worked. She was a spinster and had so loved her old cat that she couldn't bear to part with him when he passed over, so she'd had him stuffed and mounted in a glass case.

When I went into my father's shop with Mrs. Martin and her two animals and my three geese, Pat would always scold me. "Who ever heard of geese coming in a shop?" Pat would ask loudly and indignantly. "Get that lot out of here, now!" Her face turned bright red when she caught one of the geese eating a rosy red apple from one of the fruit bins that sat on the shop floor. I pretended not to hear her as first one and then the other of my geese helped themselves to choice treats. Finally, when Pat's red face was covered with perspiration and she looked ready to explode, Aunt Rene would gently ask me to take the geese outside and this I would do. When I came back into the shop, my mother always had a stern look for me, as she knew I'd been teasing poor Pat on purpose.

The escapades of my geese were nothing compared to the antics that Bertie and Jeremiah dreamed up. One day, old Mrs. Harris made the mistake of putting her shopping basket down on the floor while she went to pick out a nice, fat cabbage. No sooner had she turned her back than Bertie helped himself to the package of biscuits sitting on top of her order. Sensing he was about to be scolded, Bertie struck first, running to the large burlap sack of potatoes sitting on the floor among all the fresh vegetables and lifting his leg there.

When she saw this, Pat's eyes bugged out like chapel hat pegs, but she didn't dare say anything since Mrs. Martin was not only the vicar's wife, but also a very good customer. My father held that the customer was always right, even if their dog was ruining a perfectly good sack of potatoes with his mischief.

Mrs. Martin always brought her old baby carriage to carry her groceries home. In England we called them prams, which was short for perambulator. Jeremish rode home perched like a conquering emperor atop the groceries piled in the pram, while Bertie ran along beside, complaining the whole time and asking why he couldn't be allowed to ride as well. . . .

Jeremiah was an extraordinary cat and even more psychic than most. He once told me about a month ahead of time that a thunderstorm was coming that would damage one of the old oak tree's in the vicar's garden. And just as he had predicted, a month later a violent storm swept through the village and badly damaged one of the old oaks. I had made sure to tell Mrs. Martin when Jeremiah predicted the storm, and when it actually came to pass she was amazed. "Sunny, did Jeremiah actually tell you this?" she asked. When I told her he did, instead of saying I had a wild imagination as most of the villagers did when they heard one of my stories, Mrs. Martin kindly told me, "You have a most unusual gift, indeed." Then she turned to Jeremiah and looked him deep in the eyes. "That cat does know a lot, doesn't he?" she remarked.

As she was the vicar's wife, Mrs. Martin would often have visitors for afternoon tea. Jeremiah knew just which ones did and didn't like cats. The cat lovers he left completely alone, but he made it his business to mercilessly torment the visitors who didn't like cats. He would greet them with a loud "meow" and then rub ceaselessly against their legs. As soon as they sat down, he would spring from out of nowhere and land on their knees, giving them a start that frequently resulted in a spilled cup of tea.

When the occasion was formal and tea served in the drawing room, Jeremiah would jump up and lick the butter from the scones of the anti-cat people before they could even take a bite. Then he would scamper down to his corner and watch in amusement as the visitors were forced to eat the scones he had licked, for Mrs. Martin prided herself on her delicious homemade scones and he was careful never to commit his transgressions in her view. If someone left so much as a bite of scone on their saucer, Mrs. Martin, looking hurt, asked if they didn't like scones. So, in order to avoid offending their hostess, the poor visitors were forced to eat the scones the cat had licked. What made it even more devious was that Jeremiah was careful to direct this mischief only toward those he knew to either dislike cats or who were frightened of them.

THE annual village fete was a big occasion. The year of Queen Elizabeth's coronation, I asked Pickles if I could ride him in the parade. He liked that idea very much. I communicated to Pickles that I was going to be dressed in a very nice dress, and that he was going to have a ribbon in his harness. He immediately transmitted that he wanted a red ribbon, so I told him red it would be.

When the big day arrived, I got up early. Mr. Sturgess had told me I would have to give Pickles a bath before the parade and brush his coat until it shone. Pickles was excited about the parade and felt very happy that I was going to be riding him. I told him he was a very special horse because not many horses got to walk in the fete parade; in fact, this particular year he was the only one.

I brushed his mane and plaited his tail, telling him all the while how very smart he looked. Pickles said he hadn't had his tail plaited before, so I reminded him of the week before when I had shown him my own hair done up in a plait, and told him he would be having his tail done the same way. That pleased him immensely.

As Pickles did not have a saddle, I rode directly on his back. The old horse was used to walking with his head down to bear the weight of the baker's cart. But I transmitted a feeling to him of standing straight and tall. I told him that today he would walk with his head held high and proud, because he was my special horse.

As I rode Pickles up the road, he told me he would walk his very best and that he hoped that bad dog, Hero, who always chased him and tried to nip his legs, would not be at the parade. I told him not to worry, that nothing could spoil this day for us. I told him we were going to win the competition and when we did, I would get him a lot of apples as a reward. I told him we would get a ribbon and a nice present if we won a prize. He was even more excited about the prospect than I was.

We did get third prize and I told Pickles that I would remember the day as long as I lived. I told him I could not have won if it had not been for him, and promised to bring him apples in the field every day. Whenever we spoke of this time, he transmitted feelings of joy, love, and pride.

Looking back, one of my fondest memories is of the old horse pulling his cart through the village, with his tattered third-prize ribbon still hanging from his harness, where he insisted it stay.

*   *   *

OTHER animals often joined Pickles in our conversations. We discussed the weather, and I remember plainly how the cows complained about the rain. How they hated the feeling of misery they endured as the cold rain drizzled over them. They had no shelter, no place to get away from the weather. They told me their favorite time was when the sun was shining. You could pass the field and see them looking content, with their faces inclined toward the warm rays.

My favorite topic for discussion with my animal friends was the village news, or to put it more plainly, gossip. Some animals, the more curious ones, knew everything about everyone and were eager to tell all. They accepted the foibles of their human companions and were not judgmental, but often they had a hard time understanding the complexities of human behavior. They especially didn't understand Tappy, who was unkind to his wife and children. The cat at the confectionery told us that no matter how many times he had beaten her during the week, Tappy always bought his wife a big box of chocolates when he got paid, to make up for his rages. The cat thought it a poor exchange for a life of terror, and we all agreed.

Following these gossip sessions, I often got into trouble with my mother for knowing something I wasn't supposed to know. If I had been wise, I would have said nothing, but I was just as eager to share the village gossip with my family as the animals were to share it with me. Mother could never track down the source of my knowledge. When she asked me how I knew so much, and I told her such and such a dog or cat had told me, she just got angrier. "Little pigs have big ears," she would say just like my dad, not realizing how very true her statement was.

*   *   *

ONE day my father came home with three goose eggs and told my mother they were for me. He told me if I put them under a chicken and watched them, the eggs would hatch out. I was very happy to think I would have my own geese.

The chicken sat on the goose eggs for a number of weeks, and I made daily inspections to see if any little goslings had pecked their way out. One day I was thrilled to find one already halfway out of its shell. Then two days later the other two geese followed.

I finally felt I had my own little family. The three goslings, responding to my love and kindness, followed me everywhere. I named them after my favorite flowers of the field; Buttercup, Daisy, and Primrose. As they got older, they began to communicate with me like all the other animals. We would sit and chat for hours in the field near the henhouse.

On Saturdays, I dressed up and went with my grandmother on the bus to nearby Northhampton to help her with the shopping. I cherished these times alone with my grandmother and tried to be on my best behavior. Still, my geese walked with me to the bus stop, and waited with me until the bus came, at which point I told them to go home. My new dog, Silky, a golden retriever, accompanied the geese. When the bus pulled away, he saw them safely home.

My geese and Silky even went with me to school each day, going as far as the school gate and waiting until the whistle blew. When class started, my animals went back to the field by the henhouse. At break time they returned to share a bit of cheese sandwich with me. After break, they returned home once again and when the school day was over, I joined them there.

Some of the other children were amazed at my entourage. They thought it was strange having geese as pets, but I didn't care. With my geese, I had security and a sense that they belonged to me.

One day, the geese told me they had something special to share. Primrose, who was always in charge by virtue of being the largest and most determined of the three, marched forward, breathless with the news that Silky was going to have puppies. She had overheard my father telling Mr. Webster that news. No sooner had she relayed the information than Buttercup asked me, "What are puppies?" I explained, within the confines of my limited understanding, that puppies were baby dogs put into Silky's tummy one night by a fairy.

"How do they get out?" Buttercup asked.

"When they are ready, they just pop out," I replied. Then all three geese declared they would like to have some puppies too.

I explained further that geese didn't have puppies; they had baby geese, which came out in the form of eggs. This didn't sound nearly as intriguing as having puppies in their tummies, so they all decided to pass on the opportunity to reproduce themselves. They declared they would help Silky with her puppies when the time came.

Each evening, my geese went with me while I shut the hens up in the henhouse. I told them they had to stay in their little goose house at night for protection from the foxes. I told them foxes did bad things to geese and hens, so they listened and stayed inside their little house all night long until I came back and let them out the next morning.

THIS happy relationship continued for almost nine months. I spent idyllic days in the company of my beloved animals, chattering away with them about many interesting subjects. I told them everything—how I did in school, what were my favorite and least favorite subjects—and they listened as if I were the most fascinating child in the world. They commiserated with me about my family problems, and I listened to all their intrigues.

There was a dog in the village named Hero whom none of them could stand because he had a bad temper. They often regaled me with tales of their latest encounter with that dreadful dog, but compassionately acknowledged that Hero couldn't help himself because he had a mean human for an owner.

My animals explained to me that most humans did not take the time to talk with them as I did. Most humans, they said, could not understand them when they spoke. Though I'd had inklings of this, this was my first actual confirmation that my ability to communicate telepathically with animals was unusual.

My geese liked being in the field with their namesakes, the buttercups, clovers and daisies. I even made them daisy chains and put one around the neck of each goose and my dog too. I made one for myself as well, and people would smile at me with my menagerie of pets, all bedecked with daisies.

I remember how pleased the geese were that they didn't have to go to school. They wondered why I had to go. I told them that's just what human children did, that I had to go to school to learn. "Learn what?" they queried. "You already know everything important." They couldn't conceive of making a child sit indoors all day, away from the fields and the flowers and animals of nature. They told me they missed my company while I was in school, and longed for the hour of my return.

I remember this period as a golden time, surrounded and encompassed by the love of my animals and my grandmother Robishaw. I had a feeling of belonging with her, a feeling I didn't have with the rest of my family. I often asked my mother if I had been adopted, because I felt so different from the rest of my family. But my grandmother understood me, understood the incredible gift of animal communication I had been given, because she herself was very clairvoyant and often had premonitions.

My grandmother also helped me learn how to communicate better with humans despite my hearing loss. As a young woman, she had worked in the cotton mills at Lancashire. Normal speech was impossible because of the noise from the machinery, so the young girls who worked there learned to read one other's lips. It was this skill that Emmaline taught me, and it helped me feel more connected to the human world.

I began to realize that not all people loved animals as I did, nor harbored the same tender feelings. I wondered why so many adults believed they were superior to animals. To me, human behavior was far worse and more unpredictable than animal behavior, and I liked the animals much more than some humans (and still do).

Animals always had perfectly reasonable explanations for everything they did, and never deliberately hurt one another as the humans of my acquaintance often did. I began to realize that my ability to communicate with animals was something that no one could understand, much less believe in, except for my grandmother. Finally, my family's impatience with my "imaginativeness" began to make sense. They truly did not believe I could talk to animals. Such a thing was outside their experience.

Then came the Christmas of 1950. I came home to eat lunch after riding horses with friends at a nearby farm. It was a Sunday, and lunch was a big occasion in England—large meals with roasted meat of some sort, vegetables and stuffing to accompany the meal, and apple pie, custard or rice pudding for dessert. This particular occasion was made even grander because it was Christmas, so my mother had decided to prepare a special meal.

I walked into the house and changed for lunch, being careful to wash my hands and brush my hair before presenting myself at the table. When I sat down, my mother came in carrying a steaming platter, smiling broadly as my father announced, "We've got goose today!" Mother put the platter down on the table in front of my father so he could carve the bird, and then I realized I was looking at one of my beloved friends who had been killed and served up for this occasion.

I was stunned. I couldn't cry or speak, I was so choked with emotion. Then I felt tears running down my face, and I started sobbing. I felt like my heart had been torn in two parts. I got up and ran away from the table, out to the garden where my geese always were. None of them were there. I ran to the goose house, but they were not there, either. I looked frantically from place to place, visiting all their favorite haunts, searching desperately for the other two geese.

Finally, I went into the barn. There in full view, were my beautiful friends—dead, hanging by their feet from the rafters, blood dripping from their mouths. My father had killed all three geese, planning to give the other two as Christmas gifts to families in the village.

Raising stock for food was a way of life in the English village, particularly just after the war when meat was in scarce supply and rationing was still in force. What my father had done was routine for him and for the other members of my family. For me, it was a horror. I felt all the pain and terror the geese had felt. I sat and looked at their dead, cold bodies and sobbed and sobbed. A part of me had died with my beloved friends. The innocent happiness of my childhood had been cruelly torn away.

At that moment, overwhelmed with anguish and pain, and knowing I could not allow myself to feel this heartbreak ever again, I forced a door in my mind shut for what I thought would be forever. Though I still loved my animals and doted upon them,

I would not allow myself to communicate with them in that special way, so that I could understand their thoughts, feelings and desires, and tell them my own in return. It was to protect myself from the anguish of my little family's horrible deaths that I vowed I would never again open myself up to an animal's pain and suffering.

My grandmother helped me perfect my lip-reading skills so I could function more easily in the human world, and as I matured, I left the world of animal communication behind. For the next forty years, my determination to forget held firm.

CHAPTER TWO

Animals Tell the Best Gossip

The Beginning of My Animal Communication

*I*t was the spring of 1994, and I was tired. I was in my studio in the Galleria area of Houston, where my daughter, Emma, and I had immigrated to start a business teaching American and European etiquette. The business was going well, but I was putting in long hours to build it up.

One day, after a particularly busy morning, I went to sit for a moment on the sofa in my studio and relax with a cup of coffee. Suddenly, I thought I saw something out of the corner of my eye, so I turned to look. Above one of the large mirrors on the wall, I saw a bright white light building up in the room. I realized it was the top half of an angel with large wings. She had a beautiful and gentle face. I knew the angel was going to speak to me.

"You will be doing God's work," the angel said. "You will be working with and for animals," the angel continued, then she left.

I sat quietly, wondering what sort of work it would be. I was speechless, overwhelmed. I wondered what had just happened. I didn't know it yet, but in a matter of weeks, the channel of energy flowing between me and the animal kingdom would become so powerful it would completely override my childhood vow to shut out the voices of my animal friends.

For two weeks, nothing more transpired. I stayed so busy with my etiquette business I had little time to contemplate the angel's visit or what it meant. At home one morning, I went into my dressing room to put on my makeup and became aware of a presence behind me. Then I asked the visitor, "Who are you?" And he answered, "I am St. Francis, the patron saint of animals. I am going to be working with you to help and heal animals."

That was all the saint said. I sat down to ponder what the visitations meant. I was beginning to have faint recollections from my childhood, faded memories now struggling back to life within some forgotten corner in my mind. Something was nibbling at the edges of my consciousness—thoughts, feelings I couldn't quite yet get hold of. The door was opening a bit further, but it would still be weeks before I completely grasped the significance of my two heavenly visitations and began to understand what I know now, the course of my true life's work.

For a few weeks, I was still a bit puzzled. I tried to understand what St. Francis had meant when he told me he was going to be working with me to help and heal animals. I remembered an incident that had happened in England before I moved to America. Late one evening, my husband, Fitz, had come in and made a big fuss over our cat, Wellington, who is quite an elegant and sophisticated animal. As Wellington tried to leave the room a few minutes later, Bella, our beloved Rhodesian Ridgeback, bit him, drawing blood from the cat's neck. The attack amazed me because the animals had lived together in perfect harmony for years.

When I went to America, Fitz moved from our main house into our guest apartment. Wellington preferred to stay in the big house, which he liked to patrol, while Fitz took Bella to the cottage with him. The tenant who rented the big house loved cats and doted upon Wellington. But the attack bothered me, and it worried me to leave my pets behind.

After the first year, the tenants left and Fitz moved back into the big house, putting the two animals back together again for the first time in a while. Over in America, I started to worry after I heard this news, concerned that Bella's obvious jealousy might mean trouble for Wellington. I asked Fitz to be especially watchful once the two animals were reunited, to ensure that Bella did not repeat her attack.

I expressed my fears to a number of my friends, and one friend recommended a respected animal communicator known as Florance who lived in California. I called and told the woman my story. She promised she would try to pick up the animals the next morning after returning from church. But the communicator was concerned about the distance involved as she had never tried to communicate with an animal so far away. I reminded her that telepathic communication knew no limits of time or distance, and was surprised to discover she did not know this. Florance told me when she was ready to communicate, she just relaxed and it came to her. At that point, I wasn't even sure how I knew it, but understood intuitively that it was so. I spoke with the conviction of this belief and Florance agreed to try and get in touch with my animals to discover the problem.

The next day I rang the communicator again and discovered that she had, in fact, been able to get in touch with my pets in England. To my astonishment, we found Bella blamed herself for my departure to America, assuming I had left home because I was angry about the attack on Wellington. According to the communicator, Bella was very upset about my absence, and wanted to know when I would return to England. Wellington told Florance he wasn't bothered about Bella's jealousy; he just stayed out of her way. But he did miss me and also wanted to know when I would return.

I realized the information the woman had given me was absolutely accurate, completely typical of my two pet's disparate personalities. The incident turned a key in my mind and made me waken to some forgotten memory; I knew I could do this sort of work too.

I decided to test my own powers of animal communication. I remembered I had once been able to do this with ease, and suspected this gift was what St. Francis had been referring to when he told me I would be helping animals.

Each day at the same time, I started to speak to my animals. I visualized my home in England, and tried to speak to Bella and Wellington. I kept the conversation up for two weeks without receiving anything back, but I kept trying. I had promised myself I would keep trying for three months to see if the experiment would work.

One evening, I was booked as the speaker at a social gathering for a businesswomen's club in Houston. Just before dinner was served, I suddenly heard my dog, Bella, speaking to me telepathically.

"Why haven't you answered me?" Bella demanded. "I've been talking and talking to you and you haven't answered. Are you still angry at me because I bit Wellington?"

I practically jumped from my chair. I told my daughter, Emma, who knew I had been trying to establish contact with my pets, that Bella had suddenly come through and was talking to me and sending me pictures. It was my first realization that animals communicate primarily by transmitting pictures of what they are talking about.

"When are you coming home?" Bella wanted to know. "We all miss you. Everybody here is sad without you."

I was overjoyed to hear my dog's voice. Suddenly Wellington chimed in with all the gossip of my village back home. In his wanderings about Aston Lee Wall, the inquisitive cat had picked up the local tidbits. He told me that Daisy, an elderly woman in the village, had gone into the hospital, a fact that I verified in my next telephone conversation with Fitz. Bella then complained that the cleaning lady didn't clean the house the same way that "Mummy" cleaned it and I laughed. Bella also said Fitz was very annoyed because the car had broken down, and that she was very sad because my mother, who had been to stay for a few weeks, had returned to her own home and Bella missed her.

All this was going on in a roomful of women who were expecting, within a matter of minutes, a speech on the finer points of etiquette. I could not get over my amazement. Somehow, I had known that I could do it, that I had the gift of communicating with animals through mind energy, but I couldn't explain how I knew this. I gathered myself and stood to walk to the podium. I tried to organize my thoughts for my speech while Bella and Wellington's voices were still ringing in my mind. I thought briefly that if I told my audience of my incredible experience, some would think I was stark raving mad.

I delivered my speech, but I couldn't wait to get into the car with Emma, to discuss what had happened with Bella and Wellington.

From that time on, I talked to my animals every day. Wellington continued in his role of village gossip, while Bella tried to determine when I would be coming home. I asked them to love and take care of one another, and Fitz reported a change in the former rivals' relationship. Then one day, Bella reported being cross with Wellington because he had killed a bird and put it under a table in the house. Bella told the mighty hunter off, reminding him that I didn't like it either when he stalked birds. Fitz reported that Bella barked and barked at Wellington the day he killed the bird. I was daily becoming more convinced of the accuracy of my communication with my animals. Everything they told me Fitz confirmed, and I had no other possible way to get the information that Bella and Wellington transmitted during their daily conversations.

When Fitz relayed the story of Bella's anger with Wellington, suddenly the reason for the previous attack became clear to me. Each year, the swallows returned from Africa to nest in the old barns, stables, and outbuildings on our property. It was an event that filled us with joy, not only because of the beauty of the birds, but because their return signaled the end of the long, cold English winter, and the promise of warm, sunny spring days ahead.

We looked forward to the return of the swallows each spring, and to the birth of their babies as they nested on our land. We sat in our beautiful cottage garden each evening, surrounded by fragrant lupines, hollyhocks, honeysuckle and tree roses, enjoying a glass of wine and the soaring flight of the swallows. I knew that many of the swallows perished along the way, so I felt a special responsibility to care for the survivors who showed up faithfully in my garden each spring.

When the baby swallows were learning to fly, many of them dropped into the grass, a perfect opportunity for a marauding cat. I always tried to keep Wellington in the house during the few days the babies were testing their wings. But Wellington, like all cats, would manage to find a way out. His hunting instinct was deeply ingrained.

One day Wellington killed two baby swallows and that upset me very much. Bella heard me scolding him and became angry because she knew Wellington had done something to anger me. Unbeknownst to us, she decided to try and help with this problem. She took it upon herself to punish Wellington for his transgressions and that was the reason she went for him, not jealousy as I had incorrectly supposed. Of course, I had no way of knowing Bella's line of reasoning at the time, because I had not yet reestablished my ability to communicate with animals telepathically.

As my confidence in my ability to communicate with animals grew, I began to share with a few close friends the details of the remarkable thing that had happened to me. When I first started my animal-communication business, not many of my friends knew exactly what I was doing. They thought of me as a British etiquette expert, and there was not always a convenient time or place to tell them how my life was changing as I was led more and more toward working full-time with animals.

Then Stacey, my friend who had recommended the animal communicator in California, asked me to talk to her two cats, Hubert and Leonard, to see if I could help with a couple of behavioral problems that had developed. I agreed, feeling ready to tackle whatever assignment St. Francis might send my way. I knew I had embarked on my true life's mission.

CHAPTER THREE

Human Emotions

Your Pets Know Just How You Feel

One of the most difficult things for humans to understand is the powerful effect their own emotions can have on the behavior and outlook of their animal companions. Animals feel everything that we feel; they sense when their humans are happy, sad, discouraged, excited, or angry and react accordingly.

Frequently, when I am called to consult on an animal's problem behavior, I can trace the source of the difficulty right back to some upset or change that has happened within the family. Or, in the case of rescued animals, it may be that the change has brought back a traumatic memory from their past. When I talk to the animal and ask him what he is trying to let his human companion know with his changed behavior, I find that he will tell me. A death, a divorce, the birth of a baby, a change of house, illness, financial difficulties, conflict or deadlines at work— any of the hundred problems that can beset us—can also deeply affect our animal friends.

Remember that animals gather information telepathically. When you are worried or upset about something, an image of that worry forms within your mind and transmits out from your imagination like a radio beam. Your pet picks up all these silent communications and for him they are even more powerful than your spoken words. So even though you may think that you are hiding your thoughts and feelings from your pets, you really are not. They know everything, and if you are upset and harboring a lot of powerful negative emotions, this will surely affect your pet as well as you are transmitting those feelings out like a radio all the time, beaming pictures that you form in your mind, as well as your thoughts and feelings.

So, if you and your spouse are thinking of ending your marriage, your pet sees the images that have already formed in your mind of you living apart from your mate, and it is very confusing and upsetting to him because he does not understand human concepts like divorce. Usually, the animal loves both of you and the thought of being separated from one of you is traumatic. All they know is that their cozy situation is changing because you are both angry and unhappy, and that is very unsettling to our animal companions. It's a very sad situation for pets when a family breaks apart, but all too often, humans fail to take their animal companion's feelings into account during times of crisis like a divorce and this can lead to behavioral problems.

Many animals react to this sort of stress by acting out. Pets that have always been perfectly well-behaved will start soiling and chewing in an effort to show their displeasure with the unhappy emotions swirling through their homes. But it doesn't have to be anything as dramatic as a divorce that sets your pet off. Sometimes it can be something as simple as jealousy. If they decide you are spending too much time with the new puppy or kitten and not enough time with them, you can be sure that problems will ensue. They will find a way to let you know they are not pleased with the current situation, and then it is up to you to work out the exact nature of the problem and effect a remedy.

We humans tend to make decisions based solely upon our own needs and desires and frequently fail to take into account the needs and desires of our animal companions. Yet everything we do, every decision we make, has the potential to affect our pets dramatically. You may walk by a pet store and see a puppy that appeals to you and impulsively decide to take him home, little stopping to consider what effect this "interloper" will have on the pets you already have in your home. To prevent this sort of problem, always talk to the animal you already have in your home and ask him to help you take care of the new arrival. Remember your pet is always in tune with your energy line so you can ask him for his help right from the pet store before you even bring the new pet home.

You may decide to move to a bigger house, failing to take into account that your pet loves the park by the old house where you take your daily walks together. Or perhaps your relationship isn't working out so you decide to leave your partner, but your pet that loves you both can't understand why one of you is gone.

Does this mean you should never get a new pet, never change house or romantic partner? Of course not. It simply means you must prepare your pet for the inevitable changes and upsets that occur in our lives. Talk to him using the images and feelings in your mind, and be sure to send him feelings of love and ask for his help during the transition. This will change your pet's feelings of doubt and fear because he will no longer feel left out.

The first thing to do is to work out when the problem started because there is always a relationship between the start of the problem and the event that triggered it. For example, if your cat that has always been fastidious in his litter box habits suddenly starts going outside the box the day after you bring home your first baby, you can feel quite certain that the difficulty is connected to the jealousy and uncertainty he feels about this baby who seems to be taking up so much of your time. Always acknowledge that he is doing the soiling, then tell him you understand why it has occurred. Don't be angry with him; just love him. Look into his eyes and tell him you understand what he is telling you and he does not need to do this anymore. Then see in your imagination what you want him to do in the future.

If your dog started chewing up shoes within the week after your son leaves for college and has never done that sort of thing before, it's easy to imagine it is his response to missing the child who may have been his companion for years. The shoes have a familiar scent to them and chewing on them gives the dog comfort.

A little understanding and compassion goes a long way in such situations. Put yourself in your pet's place and try to understand what they are feeling. If you can do that, you will be able to come up with sensible solutions to whatever problems you may have with your animal companions.

The problem may be something that to you seems absolutely inconsequential, but rest assured your pet doesn't view it that way. For example, I have had clients whose animal companions became very upset simply because their owners changed what they fed them, or moved the location of their bed or basket. One dog was piqued because his groomer had switched the color of his ribbon from red to blue; another because he wanted a bandana and not a ribbon. As comical as it may seem to us, it was a very important issue to the dog who was determined to go right on relieving himself on the Oriental rug until he got his blue ribbon back. Just realizing that it really can be something as simple as this causing your pet's change in behavior can put you ahead of the game.

You may be wondering why animals are so sensitive to changes in their environment. It's because, like us, they are creatures of habit and they like their familiar comforts. When something changes, often the only way they have to let us know how they feel is to misbehave, because they know that mischief will certainly attract our attention. They don't mind what type of attention you give them, good or bad, just as long as you give them your attention. Even if their behavior has caused you to become angry, at least you are listening to them.

Animals often become confused by the difference in your spoken words and the mental images you are projecting. For example, if you shout, "Don't chew on the rug!" at the same time you are projecting out a picture of your dog chewing on the rug, how are they to choose between the two conflicting commands? Usually they go with the telepathic image because it is stronger and more readily understandable to them than the spoken word. When you see in your mind's eye your dog chewing on the rug, that is language your dog readily understands and he will chew on the rug. That is why I emphasize the importance of matching your mental images to your spoken words, to avoid upsetting your pet. Be positive with your thoughts and mental images. Picture him doing what you want him to do instead of what you don't want.

Animals are not familiar with the human concept of deceit; therefore it is imperative that you are always honest with them. If you fib to get them into their carrier by telling them they are going to the park and yet they are receiving the clear image of the visit to the vet that you actually have in your mind, they may learn to distrust you. If you always tell your animals the truth, even if it is something they may not want to hear, then they will learn that you can be trusted implicitly.

Remember that animals are very intelligent. If you take the

time to explain a given situation to them—such as why they have to go to the vet, or that you are going out of town for the weekend but you will be back in two days—they will be much more likely to settle down and accept what is happening without complaint. Always be sure to tell them how much you love them, and assure them that you have their best interests at heart and all your decisions are made with those interests uppermost in your mind. If you do this, then the love and trust between you and your animal companions will grow ever stronger.

Sadie

Sometimes pets behave badly as a show of loyalty to their owners. A friend's daughter, Meghan, had just graduated from college and moved into her first apartment with her college roommate. The girls had always had a good relationship, but after they moved into the apartment various tensions arose, and the problems only got worse after Meghan brought home a rescue dog and named her Sadie. Meghan is a great animal lover and three years in a college dorm without the company of a dog had been very difficult for her to accept, so she was most eager to have an animal companion in her life once again. Her roommate didn't dislike dogs, but simply did not have the patience that Meghan had when it came to dealing with the dog's accidents and constant chewing. Meghan enrolled the dog in an obedience class and over the course of months, with love and consistent training, Sadie turned into a delightful companion. The accidents became a thing of the past. With Meghan's love, Sadie was able to overcome her fear of people, caused by the fact that she had been so abused in her first home, and she and Meghan established a deep and loving bond and trust.

Unfortunately, things were not going as well with the roommate. She and Meghan frequently had verbal sparring matches, mostly over minor things, but the problems were grating to both girls. The cause was a simple difference in temperament, and it could have easily been worked out except that both girls were being a bit stubborn and self-righteous.

Finally came the day when there was a huge shouting match. Poor little Sadie was quaking as she listened to the shouting, then she finally determined she had to do something about it. Gathering her courage about her, the small dog marched into the roommate's bedroom where the fight was in progress, caught the attention of the roommate, and then staring her full in the face, squatted and relieved herself on an expensive decorative rug. At first the roommate was enraged, then suddenly the two girls became quite sheepish, for they realized their constant fighting was childish, and having a very bad effect on poor Sadie. They burst out laughing and were able to restore their friendship to its former comfortable state, thanks to Sadie's intervention.

It took a lot of courage for this small dog to step in between two squabbling humans, but in essence, this is what our pets are doing whenever they act out; they are trying to draw our attention to something they believe is important. She was asking them, "Please don't fight. It upsets me." That day Sadie taught both these girls a valuable lesson—love, not anger, please.

ONE of the most frequent causes of upset in our animals is that we humans are fickle beings. Often, when we get a pet, we cannot make up our minds whether or not we're going to keep it. This indecision communicates itself directly to the animal and results in a lot of misery and stress for them. Can you imagine how unhappy you would be if from day to day, you didn't know if you would be allowed to stay on in your own home or given away to someone else? Animals under this sort of strain will frequently resort to misbehaving as a way of drawing attention to themselves.

I resolved a problem for a lady on my television show whose bird was pecking out its feathers. She was unable to understand why the bird was doing this, but it communicated to me that it didn't know if it was going to be allowed to stay in the woman's home or not. The lady confessed that she was in fact undecided about keeping the bird and was surprised when I told her that the bird knew this and was pecking out its feathers as a form of protest because it loved the lady and very much wanted to stay with her. The woman immediately told me that she didn't realize what had been going on and assured me that she would keep the bird. After I told the bird that its future was secure, it stopped pulling out its feathers and they grew back as beautiful as before.

As I mentioned earlier, animals make little distinction between positive and negative human attention. Of course your animal would prefer to snuggle on your lap, but if you don't make yourself available for their companionship, they will resort to more outrageous means to grab your attention.

Lincoln

My friend Alexandra has a lovely Blue-crested Conure named Lincoln. While Lincoln is generally a very well-behaved bird, whenever Alexandra's job required her to spend long hours away from home, she would return only to find that Lincoln had shredded his "bed buddy" in her absence. (Bed buddies are small, stuffed pillows that parrots and other large birds enjoy snuggling with while they sleep.) It was his way of letting her know that he missed her company when she was gone for so long. Now, when she has to work late, Alexandra knows to remove the bed buddy from Lincoln's cage before she leaves home in the morning, and she also makes sure to spend extra quality time with him when she returns.

Animals do not understand that their misbehavior does not help them; they only know that it gets them the attention they desire from the humans they love. If your pet suddenly develops a new behavioral problem, review the events of the past few days in your household and you will likely find the key to the mystery right there, along with a solution. Just remember that our pets feel our emotions as strongly as we do and don't forget to take their feelings into account when unexpected events change the course of our lives.

Introducing a Baby into Your Household

When you have your first baby, it is the most exciting time in your life, however, the introduction of a baby into a previously tranquil household can precipitate a variety of behavioral problems with your pet. Displays of jealousy, destructive behavior, soiling, wetting, barking, hissing and even nipping can result. All too often a family gives up their beloved pet because they are fearful for the safety of the baby when all that is required is a bit of thoughtful planning in advance to make the transition a smooth one.

I always find it is easier to understand your pet's behavior and thinking if you put yourself in its place. Think how you would feel after years of being cosseted and doted upon, to be suddenly shoved completely aside in favor of the screaming, squalling bundle of energy that is a baby. It is devastating for pets when this happens because it makes them feel like they are no longer loved, and they cannot understand what they have done to fall out of favor. In a situation like this, it is natural for pets to start blaming a new baby for their perceived loss of status, and behavioral problems are sure to follow if you don't prepare them ahead of time.

Many of my clients ask me exactly how to prepare their furry friends for the arrival of a new baby. There are several things to do. First, if you have a friend who has a baby, get her to record the sounds the baby makes and then play them back to your animals. This way when the baby arrives, his cries and the other sounds that a baby makes will already be familiar to your pets. Before your bring your baby home from the hospital, send a blanket home with your husband that has been wrapped around your baby and allow your animals to lie on the blanket so that they may become familiar with the baby's scent. Finally, when you do bring the baby home, always bring your animals into the room with the baby and make a big fuss over them. Tell them how they are helping you to take care of the baby and how you could not manage without them. Then when you put the baby back down to sleep, don't make a fuss over your pets until you pick the baby back up again. If you make a fuss over them and give them treats each time you talk to the baby or have the baby in your arms, then your animal friends will come to associate the baby with good times, and they will feel joy over the baby's addition to the household because you have taken care to keep reassuring them that even though there is a new baby in the house, they are still a very special part of your life too.

Because animal babies are so much better able to care for themselves right from the moment of birth, it can be quite difficult for our pets to fully understand just how helpless human infants can be. Animals do not understand that our babies cannot walk and depend upon us for absolutely everything. When they see us fussing over a new baby they feel neglected and shut out.

Just as a child who craves his mother's company will often do something naughty to grab her attention, so too will an animal who is feeling ignored contrive some way to gain your notice.

All of these difficulties can be avoided if you take steps to include your animal companion in the excitement of the new addition to the family. First you must explain to your pets as you would to a child about the impending birth. Take care to assure them that the new arrival will in no way reduce them in your affection, while also explaining that your new duties as a parent may sometimes limit the amount of free time you have. It can also be quite helpful to ask for your pet's help in caring for the baby. Include him in the day-to-day care of the baby and thank him. Animals love to feel they are sharing in the joy of looking after a new arrival. If you assign them a role and make them feel important, your animal companions will welcome the baby just as warmly as you do. As they form a loving bond with your baby, you will find that they become quite protective of the infant.

I had one client who reported that her female cat began to act quite aggressively toward her when she became pregnant. She consulted me because she thought the change in the cat's behavior was due to her pregnancy. But when I connected to the cat's energy, I felt no jealousy, only a feeling of serious illness, nausea and weakness. I sensed that the cat had cancer and her new, aggressive behavior was her way of trying to tell her owner that something was wrong and she needed help. My client took her cat to the vet that afternoon. He confirmed the diagnosis and immediately began treatment to relieve the cat's symptoms. As the cat felt better, her aggressiveness decreased. The timing of the change in her behavior and the beginning of her human companion's pregnancy was only coincidental.

Some people make the mistake of only spending quality time

with their pets when their baby is napping. This leads animals to associate the baby's appearance with the end of playtime, and once again, jealous feelings can arise. Try instead to ignore your pet while baby is sleeping; don't play with it and don't pay it much attention. Make a big fuss over both the baby and the pet when the baby wakes up so that your pet will look forward to the baby's awakening. This will reinforce the idea that the baby is an enjoyable addition to the household.

My own daughter, Emma, just had practical experience of this idea. She recently welcomed home her first baby and my first granddaughter—our beautiful little Emily. We prepared for Emily's arrival by telling Emma's two cats, Cinnamon and Raisin, how much we needed their help to care for the baby. By the time Emily came home from the hospital, both cats were bursting with excitement and anticipation. Emma has been careful to lavish attention on the cats whenever Emily is awake. In this fashion the cats have learned to associate the baby's presence with the most pleasant time of their day. Both cats have behaved splendidly toward Emily because they regard her as a positive addition to the family instead of as an unwelcome interloper.

While this may sound strange to you at first, remember I am thinking from the pet's point of view. If you make sure to include your pet in the frenzy of activity that surrounds the months leading up to the birth of a baby, you will find them helpful and protective when you bring the baby home instead of fearful and jealous. It does not have to be an "either/or" situation. People who love their animals would find it very hard to give up their "baby in a fur coat." It is up to you to prepare your animal properly to not only accept a new baby, but also to understand that the baby is as much a part of the family as the pet. If you do this, you should have smooth sailing and find that your pet can be relied upon to help you care for and protect your baby.

TEACH YOUR CHILD TO RESPECT YOUR PETS

Families who have done a good job of introducing a baby to the household sometimes stumble when it comes to teaching that baby how to interact with pets. As babies grow and become toddlers and become more mobile, a whole new dynamic emerges in your house. Your pets have been used to having the baby confined and under control and suddenly this wild little person has the run of the house, pulling tails, upsetting food dishes and grabbing the pet's favorite toys.

Time once again for a bit of planning and intervention. If you teach your child to treat all living creatures with love and respect, you will not have any problems. But of course, you must first get your toddler through those trying years when he is exploring and learning, and *no* is his favorite word.

Make sure there is a safe place for your animal friend to go when your baby starts toddling around. If you have a crate with the door open for your animal companion, make sure the baby cannot crawl inside while your pet is sleeping as he needs to have his own private, secure space. If an animal is suddenly startled awake from sleep he will snap at whatever is near out of fear, uncertainty and surprise, never intending to hurt your child. Teach your child to respect a pet's quiet times, and if necessary, make sure your child cannot intrude upon your pet's privacy. Having a toddler in the house can be stressful for all concerned, and our animal companions need to get away from time to time and relax on their own too.

During your son's or daughter's transition from infant to toddler to young child, you must take steps to protect your pets from your child or children, just as you took steps to protect your baby when you first brought it home. First, you must never allow your child to take your pet's toys or food dishes, both for sanitary and safety reasons. Second, make it quite clear that no shouting, hitting, kicking, squeezing or tail pulling will be tolerated at all. Teach your child to handle the pet gently and lovingly, speaking in soft words to assure the pet that all is well. Remind them that sometimes a pet simply does not want to be picked up and petted and they must respect that. If your children have trouble understanding why they cannot grab the pet any time they want, tell them to put themselves in the pet's place and ask how they would feel getting scooped up willy-nilly into your arms in the middle of lunch, or dragged away while they were playing a game or watching a video? This will help your child to understand that pets have daily agendas just as people do and it is important for us to respect both their wishes and their moods.

Introducing New Pets to Your Children

When toddlers reach the point where they can stand and walk, some parents think this is the ideal time to rush right out and get a new puppy or kitten, so that the baby and the pet can "grow up together." This is a bad idea. Toddlers simply do not have the self-control or presence of mind to understand how to treat a pet properly. A young child can easily squeeze a tiny kitten or puppy almost to death in an excess of love and enthusiasm. No pet should ever be put through such a traumatic experience.

It is far better to wait until your child has reached school age to introduce a new pet. At five or six years, a child has much better self-control and a greater understanding of themselves and their strength. They also are less egocentric and have more awareness of the animal's needs and rights.

While some families insist on getting a puppy or kitten, it might be a better idea at this stage to adopt a one- or two-year-old animal from a shelter for your child's first pet. Such animals are usually already trained and are eager to find loving families. Older animals are better able to defend themselves from potential mistreatment and can also do a better job of defending your child from an outside threat such as a roving dog pack or a bully.

I recommend against getting an unusual pet for young children. Most exotic animals have quite specific care requirements, and it can be difficult for a young child to follow these routines consistently. The pet's physical and psychological health can suffer if they are not fed and cared for properly, so unless you intend to take on all the pet's requirements yourself, it probably would be wisest to choose an animal whose needs are less exacting, such as a dog or cat. This is not to say that cats and dogs don't have specific care requirements as well, only that fulfilling those requirements is somewhat easier with animals that have been domesticated for thousands of years and whose needs are well-documented. Do, in fact, teach your child how to take care of a pet, to regularly provide fresh food and water, along with daily grooming and exercise or playtime. But also understand that ultimately, you have to be the responsible one as children do become lazy and lose interest very quickly when it comes to the daily requirements of pet care as the novelty of looking after the animal wears off. As the responsible adult in the household, you must take every step necessary to ensure your pet's continued well-being.

Sometimes the problem is not between your child and your pet, but between two or more of your pets. We'll discuss practical solutions to fighting and jealousy among your animal companions in the next chapter.

CHAPTER FOUR

No Bad Pets

Fighting and Other Behavioral Problems

*P*erhaps no problem is more distressing to pet owners than when a beloved and normally well-behaved pet starts acting up in ways that are unusual. Just as upsetting is when once peaceful housemates start fighting. Many of my clients consult me with this type of problem, and they are usually so distraught it has brought them to the brink of giving up the animal for adoption or, in the case of an animal that is biting or attacking, having it put to sleep. Of course, no animal lover wants to do that.

Like all problems with animals, undesirable behavior can be solved by employing a bit of keen observation to try and determine what has upset your animal. Remember, animals are like children in that they crave our attention and affection. When they feel they are being ignored, they can certainly find ways to get the attention they desire, and they really don't care whether it is positive or negative attention. All they know is that if they misbehave, their owner who has been overlooking them will sit up and take notice of the pet. The worse the lack of attention is, the worse you can expect your pet's behavior to become.

You can tell many things about your pet's mood just by observing its body language, which is easy to read and requires no special training to interpret. If your pet's ears are down, or it goes down on its tummy and has a forlorn look about its face, you can be sure something is upsetting your animal.

You do not have to have any special gifts to observe your pet, just the ability to think about the circumstances that led up to the start of the behavior problem. When you identify an element that has changed, more than likely you have discovered the cause of the misbehavior.

Animals are concerned about any change in their household. Often pet owners make changes and important decisions without considering how it will affect their pets. Remember that pets are very sensitive to the human emotions swirling around them. It is important to tell your pets the truth about any changes in the household. Help them to understand the situation, particularly if the change is to be permanent, as in the case of a divorce or death in the family.

Even when the change is not necessarily permanent, as when a child leaves for college, it is important to let your pet know what is happening. If you fail to explain to a pet why a change is taking place, the animal has a tendency to blame itself for the problem, as in the case of my Bella, thinking her attack on Wellington was what caused me to leave home for America.

Hubert

My friend Stacey, who is normally quite sensitive to her pets' needs, called me with a problem she was having with her cat Hubert. Hubert is one of a pair of grey tabby brothers, and is somewhat temperamental and high-strung, while his brother, Leonard, is more laid back. The two cats were used to sleeping with Stacey every night. This arrangement was mutually satisfactory for both human and cats.

Suddenly, Hubert started waking Stacey around three A.M. in the morning by jumping on her chest. If that didn't have the desired effect, he would go to the mini blinds over the dresser and rattle them with his paws, almost as if he were playing a xylophone, until Stacey had no choice but to get up from the bed to stop him. She was becoming angrier with each passing night, and getting cross from lack of sleep.

In desperation, she called me and asked for help. At that point, I was still experimenting with communicating with my own animals, Bella and Wellington. But I agreed to try and help.

I was surprised at how easily I connected telepathically with the cats. I asked Hubert why he was being so naughty and waking up his mommy every night. He quickly told me he was angry because Stacey hadn't been spending much time at home lately. In fact, he said, Stacey hardly ever spent any time with them anymore, so he woke her up in the middle of the night because then he was sure he would have her full, if angry, attention, which he thought was better than no attention at all.

Hubert seemed to realize he had an attentive audience, so he continued to list his complaints. He was upset because it had been a while since Stacey had served tuna fish, his favorite food. He wanted tuna more often, he told me, and couldn't understand why they didn't have it anymore. He also was missing his little red ball, which had disappeared some time earlier, and he wanted a new ball to replace the missing one. Finally, he complained that he had a new scratching post, and he liked his old one better.

I called Stacey and told her what Hubert had told me, and she admitted that her work had been greatly occupying her attention lately. She said she arrived home late, and then, once home, was so exhausted she hadn't been giving her two cats their accustomed playtime. She was also surprised to realize she had inadvertently dropped tuna from the cats' diet. She had run out and simply hadn't had a chance to go to the store where she bought her favorite brand. She realized she hadn't served it to the cats in almost three months.

She laughed when I told her about the red ball, and told me that Hubert kept it with him constantly. Quite neat by nature, Stacey said she had thrown the ball out because it was looking so shabby, never realizing it would upset Hubert. She promised to pay more attention to the cats, and to go straight out and buy some tuna and a new red ball, and to bring back the old, favored scratching post.

I then told Stacey she had to make sure and spend adequate time with her pets on a regular basis, or the problem would persist. I also told Hubert he mustn't wake Stacey up in the middle of the night. Hubert agreed to behave himself, but only if Stacey would spend more time with him during the evening hours. He also insisted that Stacey had to give him her entire attention. That interested me. He told me that even when Stacey spent time with him, often she was in the kitchen or the bathroom attending to other business, without her full attention on him. He transmitted a picture to me of the way he wanted Stacey to communicate with him, face-to-face.

Stacey started laughing when I described the transmission, admitting she often did talk to her pets from another room while she was cooking or washing or putting on her makeup. This partial attention didn't bother Leonard at all, who was quite certain of Stacey's love and unconcerned if she missed the occasional ear scratch. But Hubert, who has a more insecure nature, simply wasn't going to put up with this lack of attention a moment longer without retaliating to let Stacey know he was upset. I told Stacey atypical behavior is one of the few ways that animals have to get their owner's attention when they don't like something that is going on.

Stacey made the requested changes, pulling Hubert into her lap for a cuddle each night. Tuna was reintroduced to the diet, and a new red ball obtained. Within a few days, Hubert's nocturnal rampages stopped and he resumed his former exemplary behavior.

It is important to make sure the time you give to your animal provides quality attention. Make sure you go down to their level on the floor or bring them into your lap, establish eye contact and give them your whole attention, petting and talking to them. Remember that animals are very sensitive to materials. They like the feel of some fabrics more than others. If the fabric of your garment is slippery or rough, your pet may not wish to lie down or sit in your lap. Cats love to knead cloth, particularly soft blankets and comforters.

Some people have a problem with cats scratching their furniture. Scratching is both natural and necessary for cats to keep their claws healthy. I am completely opposed to the declawing of cats. It is inhumane and causes horrible pain, and often produces a cat that bites, as they have no other defense after their claws are removed. This is another example of an animal behavior problem that is produced by a mistake on the part of the human.

Often scratching is a result of poor training (or no training) or the use of an inadequate scratching post. Scratching posts should be substantial, tall and wide enough to bear the weight of the cat without wobbling as he stretches his body and exercises his claws. It is important for the board to be big enough for a cat to hook its claws in the top while stretching his entire body and exercising all his muscles. Cats cannot scratch properly on a round, narrow scratching post. When that is all that is provided, cats will often prefer to scratch a sofa or chair, especially if they haven't been trained that scratching furniture is undesirable behavior.

There is a simple, humane way to train cats away from furniture. Keep a spray mister of room-temperature tap water handy, and whenever your cat scratches furniture, say "No!" sharply, spritz it with water, and take it to its scratching board. The hissing sound of the sprayer and the wet water combine to give your cat a most unpleasant experience, at least in its estimation. Eventually, they learn that the furniture is off-limits. But remember, this training will work properly only if you provide an adequate alternative scratching surface.

Pebbles

I was called by my client Luan, a lovely Chinese lady whose pets I had worked with many times. She was upset because Pebbles, one of her three cats, had suddenly forced Timmy, another of her cats, into a corner and wouldn't let him come out. Every time poor Timmy tried to leave the corner, Pebbles would attack him, biting and scratching, until Timmy had no choice but to retreat. The one time Luan tried to intervene, Pebbles had bitten her, too—a fact that amazed her, because in their seven years together the cat had never been anything other than a loving and gentle companion.

I connected to Pebbles telepathically. He was very angry. I asked him why he was upset and he sent me back a funny sensation in my nose, and a picture of Timmy. I asked Pebbles, "Why are you attacking Timmy?"

Pebbles responded quite simply, "Timmy has a strange scent. If he moves out of the corner he will make everywhere smell strange."

The explanation for the uncomfortable feeling in my nose was clear, but I still didn't know why Pebbles had bitten Luan. "Why did you bite Luan, Pebbles? You have never bitten before."

"If she had picked Timmy up, she would have smelled like him, so I bit her to keep her from picking him up," Pebbles said.

Seen from the point of view of the animal, it was all so logical. I asked Luan if she had put a new spray or powder on Timmy and she told me she'd bought a new homeopathic flea remedy because Timmy had a terrible infestation of fleas, and she was afraid to use a poison on him. I wondered when she had employed the new treatment and she told me a few days before. Then I asked her if this was when Pebbles had changed his behavior toward Timmy, and she answered that it was. Compared to most cats, Pebbles has a heightened sense of smell. I reminded Luan of a previous incident with Pebbles when he had reacted to the scent of a new perfume she had started wearing by refusing to come near her. Apparently, the odor of the flea remedy was also offensive to his sensitive nose.

"It smells okay to me," Luan said, "and it has gotten rid of the fleas."

"Well, it doesn't smell okay to Pebbles," I told her. "You did not put this preparation on him?"

Luan said she had not because Pebbles did not have a flea problem.

I then explained that the awful smell was what had upset Pebbles and caused him to attack both her and Timmy. I advised her to bathe Timmy immediately with plain water and a gentle shampoo to get rid of the smell, and also to thoroughly wash her hands. I told her not to use this remedy again.

Luan called me a few days later to explain that once she bathed Timmy and got rid of the smell, things went back to normal at her house, with the two cats resuming their close, loving relationship.

While we are on the subject of fleas, I want to mention the chemical flea poisons which are so popular. While they certainly kill fleas on contact, they are also toxic to your dogs and cats, and also some people. There are many cases where an application of a flea spray, powder, or dip has produced tragic results. These deadly chemicals accumulate in your pets' bodies, and can affect their lungs, heart, intestines, skin, liver, and kidneys. Many animals have died due to a toxic buildup of these chemicals in their bodies over a period of time.

Though Luan was certainly right to try a homeopathic remedy to combat her flea problem, Pebbles simply didn't appreciate the one she selected, so she will try others until she finds one that is suitable.

I use a simple trick to keep my house free of fleas without the use of poisons. Fleas are attracted to light, so I put a small lightbulb above a bowl of soapy water in every room. When they try to jump up to the light, they land in the water and cannot escape.

You can also sprinkle plain borax powder on your carpet. The powder penetrates the fleas' hard bodies and literally dries them out, causing their death. Leave it in place twenty-four hours and then vacuum off. Keep your pets away from the carpet while the borax powder is in place, so that they don't pick it up on their paws and lick it. After you vacuum, the carpet will be safe for them again.

Amadeus

One day I received a call from Rhonda, whose dog, Amadeus, was training to be a member of the Houston Flyball Association.

Amadeus was in danger of being cut from the flyball team because of his very aggressive behavior toward the other dogs on the team.

When Amadeus arrived at my studio with Rhonda, he walked across the room looking and sniffing everywhere, then asked me where the other dogs were. I told him there were no other dogs here. He then asked where the cats were as he lived with nineteen cats. I said, "There are no cats, just you."

Amadeus had picked up the scents of the other animals who'd been to see me. Because he was so interested in investigating all the intriguing smells, it took him quite a while to settle down. When animals are taken from their familiar environment and brought to my office, they are excited, nervous, or sometimes, even a bit upset. Since I can communicate telepathically with animals immediately through their owners' energy, I normally prefer that owners consult me without their animals present, to save the twenty or thirty minutes it usually takes for the pet to calm down and become receptive to telepathic communication. I'll make an exception when an animal is sick and needs hands-on healing, but in this case, I made the exception because I didn't know until she got to my studio that Rhonda was bringing the dog with her. Once she arrived, there was no sense in making her leave.

Rhonda told me Amadeus refused to go into the box to pick up the fly ball. I asked her to draw a chart of the actual run and tell me what duties were expected of the dog in the competition. Rhonda explained the course, but said that Amadeus attacked any other dog that came near him during the competition.

I asked Amadeus why he attacked the other dogs. He told me that at one time he had been a cattle dog on a ranch, and he didn't like the cattle bumping him. He was afraid the other dogs were going to bump him if he let them get too near. I assured him the other dogs had no intention of bumping him as the cattle had so often done, and told him the other dogs meant him no harm; that they were simply trying to do a good job in the competition.

I asked him if he wanted to compete with the other dogs and he said yes, but was unsure about what he had to do. I told him he had to go into the box and pick up the ball with his mouth. When I transmitted this picture to him, Amadeus told me he finally understood what he was supposed to do.

Then Rhonda told me he wasn't very good on the lead. I asked him why he wouldn't sit and why he wouldn't do what his owner requested when she pulled on the lead, a method of control commonly used during fly-ball competitions. Then his little sad story came out. He told me that his former owner tied him up very tightly with thin string that cut into his neck, and it had hurt him very badly. He had been pulled along with the string and tied to a tree with it. His neck had been rubbed raw and was very sore. Although he knew Rhonda would never hurt him because she loved him very much, each time she pulled him a certain way, it reminded him of the pain he had experienced in the past and it confused him.

I repeated the story to Rhonda, and she told me how Amadeus had been taken from his previous owner because he had been treated so badly. She had adopted him from the Humane Society, and she did not know much about his background, but now she understood why the problems had occurred. She asked me to tell Amadeus she would not pull hard on his lead again.

During our conversation, Amadeus told me many other things that made my heart bleed. The cruelty that had been inflicted upon him was tremendous. He told me he always wanted to stay with Rhonda and never leave her for another home. He'd had several owners and was worried about moving again. I assured him that Rhonda would never leave him, and that he would never again be treated so cruelly. I also told him he was a very clever, smart dog and that he would do very well at the fly-ball competition.

I asked Rhonda to call me the night before the competition so I could go over everything with Amadeus to remind him what he had to do. After the event, Rhonda called to say Amadeus had gone into the box, picked up his ball, and behaved very well on his lead. He hadn't bitten any of the other dogs.

Things went well for a few weeks and then Rhonda called and asked me to speak to Amadeus again. The day before he had finished the fly-ball competition and done everything right. He was walking away when suddenly, for no apparent reason, he went after another dog and bit it. Rhonda was upset because the other dog's vet bill had cost her two hundred dollars.

I tuned in to Amadeus and he told me he didn't want the other dogs coming near him at the end after he'd finished, and that's why he went for them. I told him that was very unkind, and that he must not attack the other dogs; otherwise he would be removed from the team and not be allowed to compete again. I told him Rhonda would keep him apart from the other dogs as best she could.

Before the next competition, Rhonda called and asked me to remind Amadeus not to attack the other dogs. I tuned in to Amadeus and suddenly I felt great sadness and worry. I asked him what was wrong and he told me one of their cats was very sick and was dying. Amadeus wanted to know where the cat would go if it died. I often find when animals have been abused they equate dying with going to another cruel home. I reassured him, and told him that dying means the cat's spirit would go to another place where he would be very happy. I explained how the body wears out and feels pain and that the spirit must leave the worn-out body and move on. That's what dying is, I told him.

Rhonda confirmed that one of the cats was sick. I told her Amadeus was really too upset to talk at that point because unlike humans, animals can only think of one thing at a time. The cat's illness had Amadeus too preoccupied to allow effective communication. This was not the day to speak to him; he needed a week or so to get over this.

A few weeks later I was able to talk to Amadeus again and I told him it upset Rhonda very much when he attacked the other dog. Amadeus told me he didn't like the smell of the other dog very much, so he bit him. I told him it made Rhonda very sad when he misbehaved and was unkind to other dogs. Amadeus wanted to do everything correctly. He wanted to work closely with Rhonda and he wanted to get the course right. I reassured him he was a beautiful clever dog, much too smart to bite other dogs. He agreed he would behave in the future and there have been no further problems since that time.

I often find that when people have rescued pets, problems crop up that relate to incidents in the animal's early life, before the current owner came along. It takes a lot of love and patience to determine the origin of these "leftover" problems, but like any other animal behavior problem, if we can put ourselves in the place of the animal and try to look at the problem from its point of view, often we can hit upon the proper solution.

WE have discussed some ways that animals can misbehave when they are feeling neglected or misunderstood. Next, I will discuss the one problem that makes pet owners most unhappy: when an animal that was once trained begins to have accidents or does not use the litter box. Litter box and soiling problems are among the most difficult challenges pet owners face, but there are always reasons for such problems, as we shall see in the next chapter.

CHAPTER FIVE

Litter Box Blues

Housebreaking and Litter Problems

*P*erhaps nothing is more upsetting to pet owners than animals that have problems with housebreaking or using the litter box. It is difficult enough having to scoop and wipe and scrub every time you turn around, but when you consider the damage to your home, carpet, furniture and clothing, such accidents can cost a tremendous amount of money.

All these difficulties combine to make housebreaking and litter box mishaps among the leading reasons people seek my advice. The problem is especially unsettling when a pet that has been house-trained suddenly starts soiling. I always find the animal has a very good reason for these accidents, and that usually it is their way of communicating their displeasure with a particular situation that has developed in their home. Only rarely does a medical condition turn out to be the cause.

I also find the problem is more frequent with cats. Sometimes it may take a while to get puppies completely housebroken, but once they are, they don't generally have accidents unless they are ill or are left unattended for too long a period. Cats, however, are very sensitive when it comes to their litter boxes, and changes we may consider insignificant can throw them completely. Often cats show their disapproval of a particular situation by relieving themselves outside of their box.

It is important to remember that animals vary in their habits just as children do. Some puppies learn within a matter of months, while others may need up to a year before they really understand that they must perform their bodily functions outside the house. By the same token, some dogs may go right away after being taken outside, while others must sniff every bush for a mile before finding a suitable location.

You must be patient with your dog's or cat's particular style. Remember that we humans always have a bathroom nearby, while animals must rely on us to determine when they need to go outside. Also be mindful of giving your pet enough time to conduct his business. I've known of owners who herd their dogs out the front door and then start scolding them to hurry up ten seconds later because they don't want to miss a football game. Can you imagine how distressing it would be if someone yanked you up just as you were getting settled in the bathroom? Give your pet plenty of time to sniff about and find just the right location.

Some owners are negligent about taking their pet out frequently enough, then become angry with an animal that has soiled after being confined to an apartment for hours on end with no break. I had a client who was having a problem with her grown dog soiling during the day. But when I visited I learned that the lady did not let the poor dog out all day long. Of course it had accidents! Once again, it was the owner at fault, not the pet.

According to the American Veterinary Association, this type

of problem is the top reason why pets are given up for adoption by their families, and also the number one explanation given by families asking a vet to euthanize an animal that is not ill.

I abhor the idea of a pet being put down simply because of a house-training problem. It breaks my heart when animals are penalized simply because their owners have failed to shoulder the responsibilities of pet ownership. Animals must be trained to do what you want them to do, and the training must be done with love, compassion, and a great deal of patience.

Still, I understand how upsetting accidents can be to owners. We all want our homes to be pleasant and comfortable, and constant wetting will absolutely ruin a carpet. There comes a point when pet urine seeps down into the carpet padding and the smell simply cannot be removed. Then you have no choice but to replace the carpet or live with the unpleasant smell. Defecation presents its own problems. If the animal is regular, scooping up the mess presents little difficulty. But if it is suffering from loose bowels, a permanent stain can result.

Clients often ask me why their animal is having accidents. Such difficulties are never the animal's fault, but can always be traced back to something the owner is doing or not doing that is upsetting to the pet. House-training accidents are one sure way your pet can grab your attention. In the case of neglected pets, they would much rather have the negative attention that comes with the scolding over the accident than none of your attention at all.

With a bit of observation and perhaps even a little detective work, you can almost always discover the reason your pet is soiling, and then take appropriate steps to remedy the problem.

As with all pet problems, there are logical reasons for the accidents. Many times a change in routine or the family is responsible. Often the problem can be something as simple as a change in diet, litter or the location of the litter box, which can upset and confuse the animal and take it out of its usual routine.

If you can think back over the week preceding the start of the accidents, try to isolate anything different in your pet's routine. Have you changed their food or schedule, or bought them a new dish? Is there a new animal (or human baby) in the house? Has a family member been ill or away? Has there been unusual stress or discord in your home? Have you been overworked and unable to pay your pet its normal share of your attention?

Animals can react very badly when they sense that their humans are upset, and one of the first ways their own unhappiness manifests itself is usually with a soiling accident. It is an animal's way of raising a red flag and saying, "I don't like what is going on here."

Animals know soiling is not desirable behavior; that is why they often try to hide their misdeeds. Pets love their humans and want more than anything to please them, so you can be sure if an animal is deliberately engaging in a behavior they know will upset you, it is for what they consider to be a very good reason.

We must also remember that animals, just like humans, have very different personalities. We tend to think, "Well, this is what I want my pet to do, so he must do it," without making any allowances for the animal's individual preferences. For example, there are some people who think nothing of drying off with a towel someone else has just used, while others would never do that. Animals also have their peculiarities and we must make allowances for those. In a multi-cat household, some cats will use a litter box all the other cats are using; but many cats absolutely will not. Cats are very clean animals, and it is important to them to have a clean place to perform their bodily functions. If you are negligent about keeping their litter tray fresh and scooped out, don't be surprised if your cat finds another place to go to the bathroom. You must stop this tendency immediately, because once a cat decides on a place to use as its "bathroom," it is difficult to change its mind. You must train your kitten to go where you want it to go, and be diligent about keeping the litter tray clean, so as not to give your cat the idea it must go elsewhere.

The same is true of litter box location. Cats are creatures of habit. You may decide to move their litter box because it suits you, but the cat is used to having it where it has always been and will more than likely continue going to the bathroom in its accustomed spot, whether or not the litter tray is there. While some cats don't mind a change of location and will follow their litter box around, you would be surprised how many cat owners call me with complaints about accidents who answer yes to my first question, "Have you just moved the litter box?" If they answer yes, I tell them to simply move the litter box back to where it was, no matter how inconvenient it may seem, and this solves the soiling problem.

Also, don't shut your cat in too close a space. I have had many clients consult me about litter box problems who have followed the current trend and bought fancy domed litter boxes. Though the dome may keep litter from spraying, it tends to make some cats feel very claustrophobic, while others don't mind the enclosed space at all. In cases where the cat started avoiding the litter tray once the dome appeared, all the soiling problems were resolved once the owners removed the dome from the litter box and gave their cats a little breathing space.

Animals are very vulnerable when they are "doing their business," so they tend to be a bit more jumpy at this time. Just last week, a friend's cat, a wise old veteran of fifteen years, was relieving himself in the backyard early one morning. He let his guard down for a moment, and there, in the middle of a sub-urban neighborhood, a fox jumped out of the hedge, grabbed the cat, and broke its neck before my friend could chase it away. So try to be a bit more understanding if your pet doesn't like to "perform" in the open.

Once you determine what factors may have changed in the week preceding the change in behavior, you can formulate a plan to try and eliminate the cause of the accidents. It may take a bit of time to solve the problem, but your pet is worth it. If you find you really cannot get the problem corrected, you may allow the animal to live outdoors as long as you have a spacious, secure and sheltered place for him. If you do not, it is your responsi-bility to try and find a good home for your pet. Euthanizing a pet that is having accidents is entirely unacceptable, and most vets of my acquaintance will not do it. But they tell me they get many requests for such services from pet owners who thought the fluffy little kitten or adorable puppy was just going to take care of itself without any training or input from the owners at all.

Neither animals nor children can raise themselves properly, so if you do not think you can make the commitment of time, love, and energy it takes to turn an "animal" into a proper pet, it is just as well if you don't get a pet at all. You will save yourself a lot of trouble and some dog or cat a lot of heartbreak. If however, you are willing to invest yourself in training your pet to be a good companion, please continue reading, and I will share some stories of pets whose soiling problems I was able to correct.

Misty

I had an unusual case presented to me by my client, Kerry. Whenever she was at home, her cat, Misty, used the litter box consistently. But when Kerry left home, the cat used the rest of the house as a sort of giant litter box. Needless to say, neither Kerry nor her family were pleased with this turn of events.

At first I thought it was just a case of Misty being spoiled and wanting her mistress to stay home all the time, a situation that can often be remedied by the addition of another cat to keep the first cat company (see the story of Whiskey in chapter 6). But once I connected telepathically to the cat, I came to understand Misty had experienced some sort of tremendous fright months before while still a kitten. Kerry was away from the house and just as Misty was entering her litter box, she heard a tremendous crash of thunder and saw a bright lightning flash. Misty associated the terrifying boom with two things; her attempt to use the litter box and Kerry's absence. Whenever Kerry was around to protect her, Misty felt it was safe to use the litter box. But once she left the house, the cat was afraid the thunder would return if she tried to use the box.

I told Misty it was alright, that the same thing was not likely to happen again, and that the thunder and lightning could not hurt her while she was in the house. To give Misty a sense of control and empowerment, something she sorely lacks, I asked where she wanted her litter tray placed. Misty answered that if it could be placed in the closet where she liked to sleep, she would feel safe in there.

When I told Kerry about the thunder and lightning, she confirmed there had been a big storm several months previously when she was away from home. When she returned that evening, she found Misty cowering in her closet, and the litter box problems began the very next day. Kerry said that Misty spent most of her time hiding in the closet and many of the accidents occurred there.

Now we had the key to the solution of the problem, but I

was concerned when Kerry told me about Misty hiding out all the time, because occasional thunder and lightning did not seem to me to be enough of a reason for the cat to be so frightened. I decided to wait and see what would happen. Sure enough, after Kerry moved Misty's litter tray to the closet as requested, the cat went without a problem for a few weeks.

Then Kerry called me again. Misty was once again having problems, even with the litter box in the requested location. When I connected to the cat again, I asked her what else was going on that was frightening her and making her have accidents. She was very hesitant to talk to me, but after much prodding, she told me her "daddy," Kerry's husband, had been throwing his shoes at her when she was hiding in the closet and deliberately hitting her with them. His anger frightened her so badly she lost control of her bowels and had an accident, which enraged him even more. Misty was so terrified of Kerry's husband that she hid in the closet whenever he was in the house, but he had discovered her hiding place, and seemed to enjoy cruelly teasing the poor animal.

It is always difficult for me to have to tell a client that one of their family members is abusing their pet, and that this is the source of their animal's difficulties. You can imagine what an impossible situation it puts my clients in when they confront the miscreant with the information. They always demand to know who "told" on them. It is hard to explain to someone who is not sympathetic to animals that the animal itself "told."

Of course, I could not tell Kerry to choose between her cat and her husband, but that is often what I would like to tell people. When I find out from animals that their owner's spouse or sweetheart is being cruel, I want to shout, "You will never be happy with someone who does not love animals as you do."

Kerry tearfully confirmed what Misty had told me, and said

that her husband disliked the cat, particularly since it had started soiling, and often threw his shoes at it. I told her she had to protect her cat from her husband, and if she could not, then she must find another home for it.

Sadly, Kerry called several months later to say she had put Misty down. Her husband had given her an ultimatum and she gave in. If she had just taken the trouble to find a new home for Misty, I know the difficulties would have cleared. All the poor cat needed was a home filled with love and compassion. She was so frightened that she rarely left her closet. Though it is sad that Kerry chose to sacrifice her cat, it comforts me to know Misty is in a better place now where she will not suffer anymore.

Misty's case is not that unusual. I have worked with many animals that were particularly sensitive to electrical storms. Storms are extremely upsetting for some animals, while others sleep peacefully through the worst thunder and lightning. It has to do with the individual animal's sensitivity to the electromagnetic fields of the earth. If they are very sensitive, electrical storms can actually cause them physical pain. I have felt it in my own body when I am linked telepathically to a sensitive animal. It is not just the noise of the thunder; there is much more going on. A sensitive animal actually serves as an electrical conduit when storms are nearby, and as you can imagine, this is terribly frightening for them. Think of how you jump in the winter when you touch metal after building up a static electrical charge. The same thing happens to animals.

Be aware of what your animal may be experiencing. Just because you cannot feel anything, don't assume your animal cannot. Our bodies don't operate at the same electrical frequencies as animal bodies, therefore our senses are not as attuned as theirs to changes in the electromagnetic fields.

I have found that some animals can feel the electrical impulses from a human body as well. If you approach them too quickly, this will cause them discomfort, so please be aware this may be what is causing a dog or cat to pull back from you. It's not that they are unfriendly; they are simply trying to protect themselves from your electrical charge. If you have a pet that reacts to people in this way, just tell your guests to ignore him. He will come around in his own time and own way, when he feels comfortable about doing so.

If you know your animal is sensitive to electricity, try not to leave him alone during a storm, and especially avoid leaving him outside. If your pet wants to go under a bed during a storm, let him. It will help him to feel safe, and the stillness and the enclosed space will guard against the buildup of a static charge. The fright your animal feels after experiencing an electrical shock may cause him to lose control of his bowels or bladder and have an accident, so be particularly sympathetic if you find your pet has soiled on a stormy day.

Sparky

Celia came to me because her dog, Sparky, had taken to making a daily deposit near her new boyfriend's shoes and clothes after he left them on the floor beside the bed. Her boyfriend had ordered Celia to get rid of the dog or he himself would depart, but she didn't want to lose either her human or her canine companion.

Celia and Sparky had been together for ten years, ever since Sparky was a puppy. Celia said the beautiful Dalmatian had never had an accident in all that time, so I suspected that Sparky was either jealous of the attention his mistress was paying her new boyfriend, or didn't like the boyfriend and had fallen back on an age-old device to show his disapproval.

When I connected telepathically to the dog, I found Sparky was greatly distressed because he thought the boyfriend treated him unkindly. He was also, as I suspected, jealous and did not like having the man living in the house because he was used to having Celia all to himself. He missed their evening romps and was desperate for a bit of Celia's attention. Sparky was lonely and afraid. He was used to sleeping in Celia's bedroom every night and now found himself shut out, replaced by the unsympathetic boyfriend who kicked him and treated him cruelly whenever Celia was out and he was alone with the dog. The dog told me the man had threatened to hurt him repeatedly, and taunted him by saying he would get rid of him sooner or later.

Celia was worried about her dog and didn't want him to feel entirely neglected, so she had started letting him into the bedroom early each morning. Sparky seized upon this as a prime opportunity to show his disapproval of the boyfriend by performing his bodily functions on or near the man's shoes and on his clothing, something which he had never done before. He emphasized to me that he had always been a very clean dog and his bodily functions were regular, so I knew the "accidents" were deliberate. When I asked Sparky why he was soiling, he told me he repeated this behavior most mornings hoping Celia would understand why he was doing it.

But of course, she didn't. Her heart and emotions were tied up with the new boyfriend and she couldn't understand why her reliable old pet had suddenly started misbehaving. Her boyfriend was enraged and had issued the standard, "It's him or me," ultimatum.

I shouldn't have any difficulty making such a choice; the pet would always win. If you are an animal lover, it is important that your partner loves animals too or you will surely face difficulties ahead.

Though Sparky had excellent reasons for his misdeeds, I never encourage pets to continue misbehaving because it only serves to aggravate an already tense situation. When I told Celia that Sparky had told me her boyfriend treated him badly, I gently pointed out that she could never be truly happy with someone who was not as great an animal lover as she was. I told her she had to take steps to protect Sparky from her boyfriend and make him feel as special to her as he did before the boyfriend came into her life. Then and only then would the accidents stop.

Not surprisingly, that was not the answer Celia wanted to hear, so she left my studio. Somehow, she expected me to wave a magic wand and cure all her difficulties. But as all my clients soon discover, they have to work at resolving their problems with their animals, because difficulties never resolve themselves. There are no easy cures.

I hoped for the best, but felt that poor Sparky had seen his last happy days. I knew he wasn't going to stop his accidents because he was trying to make a point. I was afraid Celia would get rid of her old friend.

But there was a happy ending this time. Three months later, Celia returned unexpectedly and told me she had finally broken up with her male companion. It turned out her dog's opinion of the rejected suitor was the correct one; it just took her a bit longer than it took Sparky to figure it out. The man had been gone just a week, and Sparky was still making his daily deposits in the spot where once the man had thrown his clothes. Celia wanted me to speak to Sparky to assure him the boyfriend would not be coming to live in the house again.

I connected to the dog and gave him the happy news, and Celia has since reported that Sparky is now accident-free once again. Celia learned something from the experience and has decided she will never get serious about a man again before determining whether or not he loves animals.

Another lady came to me because her three dogs were having accidents on her carpet, a problem which had developed since the introduction of a fourth dog into the household. We solved her problem, but not until we had sorted out the hurt feelings and fears of abandonment the three older dogs experienced as a result of the new dog's presence in their home. Since accidents are often the result of jealousy and upset over the presence of a new animal, I will present solutions for this problem in the next chapter.

CHAPTER SIX

When Whiskey Met Sally

Introducing New Animals to the Household

P et owners often run into unexpected trouble when a new pet is brought into the household. The introduction of a new animal can wreak havoc upon a formerly quiet domestic scene. It upsets the pecking order of the animals already in the home, and everything must be sorted out before peace can reign again. It is most important that the pets you already have do not feel displaced by the newcomer. At the same time, you must make sure the newcomer does not get left out and feels truly welcome in your home. It is a delicate balance to achieve.

On the other hand, sometimes the addition of a new animal solves problems that may be related to loneliness, depression, or skittishness on the part of a solitary animal. If you work long hours and leave your pet alone, loneliness may lead him into mischief. The addition of another animal to a situation like this will often relieve the unhappiness of the solitary pet and put an end to the behavioral problems.

Pet owners are making a big mistake when they bring new animals into the house without informing the animals already in residence that a newcomer is arriving. I tell all my clients never to assume their pets do not have a point of view about additions to the family, because they do. I stress the importance of communicating the news to your animals *before* the new animal arrives. Ask their permission to bring another pet in. It may seem silly, but including your pet in the decision-making process by discussing his new role with him ahead of time prevents many problems.

Emphasize how much you love your pet, and how important a role he plays in your family. This is very important, as one of their greatest fears is that the newcomer may oust them from their favored place. Like a child who reacts badly to the birth of a sibling, an older pet may feel shoved aside by a newer, younger and possibly more beautiful animal's arrival in the home he once considered his alone. No matter what, a newcomer inevitably alters the balance of power among the animals. You should be sensitive to your pet's feelings and make sure to give him his accustomed shows of affection. If you fail to spend time with your older pets after a new pet arrives, your old pets are likely to blame the newcomer for the neglect, and problems will result.

The stress and conflict associated with the introduction of a new animal can actually cause your pet to become ill. That is what happened with Zuki, an iguana that was brought to me at the point of death.

Zuki

Since I started healing animals, I have worked with many different types of creatures, dogs and cats of course, but also birds, horses, and turtles. But Zuki was my first iguana.

Zuki arrived in my studio concealed in a duffel bag. He had

been so ill his owner, Karen, was afraid to open the bag because she thought he might already be dead. When I lifted him from the bag, he was limp and completely unresponsive, yet my first thought was that he was one of the most beautiful creatures I had ever seen. Neither Karen nor a succession of veterinarians had been able to discover what was wrong with him. Zuki would not eat and had grown progressively more lethargic over the previous ten days.

I put a soft, clean towel across my lap, lifted the iguana out of the bag and put him down on the towel. Zuki was still a baby, not more than eighteen inches long and less than two years old. As always, I took a few minutes to feel the animal's energy and get it used to me. As I stroked Zuki, I told the iguana what I was doing and asked his permission to help him. I waited until I felt my healing guide put the healing energy through my hands, then I put my hands gently upon him and stroked his head.

I started to get a sensation of extreme discomfort in my stomach and felt there was a blockage in the iguana's intestinal area. I was given a blue light to use and drew it from the tip of Zuki's nose to the tip of his tail, all the while visualizing the healing light going through him. I realized my guide was going to have me perform psychic surgery. I then visualized using the laser to cut Zuki's stomach open, and I could see that it was quite sore inside. I put more healing energy through his stomach, then saw the energy clearing the blockage and going through Zuki. I closed the stomach, rested my hands on the iguana, and felt vibrations in my hands as healing energy passed through them. After another ten minutes of healing, the iguana passed the intestinal blockage onto the towel, and I was very happy I had thought to cover myself before picking Zuki up!

I continued to heal Zuki until I felt energy flowing freely through him. After being listless and still for more than a week, the iguana suddenly started to move and his eyes were brighter. Karen couldn't believe the iguana had completely recovered in such a short time, and thought it was nothing short of a miracle. She was overjoyed to see Zuki so active, especially when he indicated he wanted to climb down and explore the studio.

I was curious to see if I could easily communicate with the iguana; I wondered if he was as observant and intelligent as the rest of the animals I worked with. He did not disappoint me. As Zuki continued to improve, he began to communicate rapidly.

As animals often do when they are feeling better and realize they have an audience, Zuki started to gossip about his family. He told me Karen's daughter, Shannen, had just changed her hair. When I relayed this, Karen and Shannen said it was true. Zuki also told me he had been moved from Shannen's bedroom into another room, and he wished to go back as he enjoyed the feeling of companionship he shared with Shannen, who was his special favorite in the family.

Zuki then told me he had been given something horrible to eat. Karen thought for a moment, then told me it was tofu. Zuki promptly told me he didn't want any more of that, that iguanas didn't eat tofu, and Karen agreed not to offer it anymore. Zuki then returned to his favorite topic, Shannen, and told me when he lived in her room he used to enjoy watching her. He said she often read in bed and that her bedroom was very untidy, which made her mother cross. "Absolutely true!" Karen cried out.

Zuki also said the girl often left her mug and plates at the side of the table. He couldn't understand why Karen got angry over this. He couldn't see that it mattered, and thought it was strange to get angry over something like that. He kept emphasizing how much he wanted to go back into the bedroom with Shannen, who he said talked to him all the time and made him feel special and important.

By this time, we were all laughing out loud and Zuki was getting perkier and perkier. I had never seen such a remarkable recovery. He told me our conversation had made him feel much happier.

Then Zuki really began to open up. He told me there was another iguana in his house who had been cruel to him. I suddenly picked up the other animal, named Spika, who started to talk. I was amazed at the intensity of the creature's jealousy toward little Zuki. Spika did not like Zuki at all and proceeded to tell me in no uncertain terms he wanted Zuki to die and go away. I realized part of Zuki's illness was caused by the stress of the other iguana's intense jealousy. Karen, from her human point of view, thought the two iguanas would enjoy being close to each other. On the contrary, I found the animals disliked each other intensely.

The main source of trouble turned out to be a glass enclosure, which had originally been Spika's. Spika had outgrown the enclosure and had been given a splendid new cage to accommodate his size. Karen had then given Spika's old cage to Zuki.

But to Spika's way of thinking, his favorite cage had been thoughtlessly taken away without regard to his feelings. It didn't matter that he could hardly fit in the cage any longer. He couldn't see it from the standpoint of practicality. Spika felt only intense jealousy, because he believed he had been unfairly removed from his cage so that Zuki could have it. I also discovered Spika did not like to share the attention his family had formerly lavished solely upon him.

After Karen placed the two cages into the same room, Spika took advantage of their proximity to torment poor Zuki. Zuki felt intimidated by the older iguana, and completely subject to his power. The powerful negative energy vibrations Spika constantly sent Zuki's way were actually what had made the little iguana ill.

I'm sure you've all heard of voodoo. What Spika did to Zuki was comparable to that ancient practice; he made Zuki believe he was going to become ill and die, and the power of that suggestion made Spika's heartfelt wish become Zuki's unhappy reality. He really believed it when the other iguana told him he didn't want him there anymore and that he was dying.

I told Karen to separate the iguanas' cages so they could not see each other, which would put Zuki well away from Spika's negative energy vibrations. I asked her to put Zuki's cage back with the daughter who loved him, as he always enjoyed the girl's company in the past. Karen readily agreed, so I reassured Zuki he would not have to see the other iguana again, which made him very happy.

The intense jealousy Spika directed constantly at the little iguana had broken down Zuki's immune system, making him vulnerable to illness, and more and more despondent. The joy of hearing he would not ever have to see his jealous rival again proved the best medicine of all for Zuki.

Back into the duffel bag went Zuki, now happy and healthy, for the journey home. As he was tucking his head down, he poked it up one last time and asked me to have Karen raise the temperature in his tank as he liked it a bit warmer. I promised I would tell her. When Zuki returned home, his tank was immediately moved back into Shannen's room. Karen reports that Zuki happily watches Shannen for hours on end.

Much of this difficulty could have been avoided by communicating with Spika prior to Zuki's introduction to the household. There is no doubt in my mind Spika would still have been jealous, because that was part of his personality. But it certainly would have lessened the intensity of his angry feelings if he had been reassured beforehand about his ongoing role in the family, his importance and the love the family had for him. It did soothe Spika somewhat when I told him the reason his cage had been taken from him and given to Zuki was not a punishment as he had supposed or to show favoritism to Zuki, but simply to accommodate his growth. But I suspect Spika will always be jealous of Zuki.

Hubert

After several idyllic years as Stacey's fondest companions, my old friends Hubert and Leonard, introduced in chapter four, found themselves in charge of two young kittens. Because their owner, Stacey, had asked their permission to bring the kittens into the house, they did not feel jealous or cause any problems. But there is still a funny story to be told here, a story that illustrates the wisdom of including your pets in the decision to add new animals to your home.

The funny part is about Hubert. As we already know, Hubert is high-strung and quite self-determined. We rarely could make him give up a bad habit unless we could show him how he could benefit from acquiescing to our request. But in the face of parental responsibility, Hubert did an about-face. He decided to give up his old ways and become a perfect role model for the kitties.

Stacey had bought a nice scratching post, which Hubert steadfastly refused to use, much preferring to sharpen his claws on his old favorite spot on Stacey's sofa. We had made little progress toward a resolution of this problem despite several conversations with Hubert. But after I told him he must set a good example for the new kittens and show them how to behave properly,

Hubert became a new cat. He took his role very seriously, and Stacey reported he could be seen stretching and exercising his claws on the scratching post whenever the kittens came near— the perfect adult feline role model. No more sofa-scratching for Hubert, and certainly none for the kittens in his charge.

The next time I connected to Hubert through Stacey's energy, I congratulated him on his progress toward responsibility. He told me that once he found himself in charge of teaching the kittens the right way to behave, he realized he himself couldn't be seen behaving badly, and so he changed his old habits accordingly.

I like Hubert's story because it is a good example of the positive things that can happen when a new animal is properly introduced to a multi-pet household. When you take pains to make sure your old pets still feel loved and important, and emphasize to them that the newcomer will serve only to make the family even happier, you can stop problems before they start.

Murphy

My client Pam took no such precautions. She brought a beautiful new dog into her home without thinking of the effect it might have on the dog she already had. Her family showered such lavish attention on the newcomer that their old dog felt quite left out. When he started to attack the new dog in an attempt to draw some attention back to himself, the poor dog found it had quite the opposite effect from what he desired. His formerly loving family turned on him for being cruel to the new dog. What they didn't understand was that the attacks were his way of expressing his dismay at their almost total neglect of him.

My involvement in the story began when Pam came to me and said she'd had to drop her dog Murphy off at a veterinary clinic, where the animal was being boarded for the day while Pam was in Houston. I asked her why she needed to take Murphy to board if she was just going to be away for the day. Pam said it was because Murphy kept attacking her other dogs, and he was in a terrible state with all his hair coming out. He was almost bald.

I felt an overwhelming sense of compassion for Murphy, so I asked Pam if she would like me to see if I could tune in to Murphy and find out why he was attacking the other dogs. I explained to Pam that there always had to be a reason for an animal's misbehavior, and that perhaps I could help her sort out the problems with the dogs in her household.

Without questioning me further, Pam said yes, she would appreciate any help she could get with the problem as it was causing great distress in her family.

When I connected to Murphy through Pam's energy, a very sad little voice came through, and I realized the dog was terribly upset. He told me he was brokenhearted because his family was going to give him away. When I relayed this to Pam, she looked at me absolutely astonished and said she'd only just asked her maid that morning if she would take Murphy, because the maid loved Murphy very much, and Pam was fed up with the problems that Murphy was causing. I explained to Pam that animals understand everything we are saying. Still, the remark made that morning was the result of weeks of Murphy's misbehavior, so I hadn't gotten to the bottom of the mystery yet. Pam's request to her maid was the end, not the beginning of the matter.

Murphy then told me that Pam's daughter had called him ugly. That made him sad because once he had been a beautiful dog, but as his hair had mostly fallen out, he knew he wasn't beautiful anymore. Hearing Pam's daughter call him ugly just added to his pain.

When I told Pam this, she said, "Oh, we do call him ugly, but only as a joke! We didn't realize he knew what we meant!"

Pam was devastated at the hurt the family's thoughtless joke had caused her little dog. She went on to tell me that Murphy was the family's first dog, and she had always had a special fondness for him before the trouble started.

Murphy interrupted to say his family had him first before any other dogs came into the house, and that he always felt very beautiful and very special to his family. Then Pam decided to add to her dog family. She bought two more dogs, and the new dogs had puppies, including one with soft fur and beautiful eyes they called Charlotte. Pam decided to keep Charlotte in addition to her other three dogs.

Soon after, Murphy began to feel neglected. He felt all the attention was on Charlotte, whereas it used to be on him. Learning to share the attention and affection of their masters can be just as difficult for animals as it is for human brothers and sisters, particularly when they have been the center of attention for some time before the newcomer appears.

Murphy told me that Charlotte and her mother and father would not speak to him at all, and this made him feel very sad and lonely. Murphy started attacking Charlotte, and the attacks had grown so vicious that Pam was forced to separate the two dogs. Pam was at a loss as to what caused the trouble, since the dogs had been getting along beautifully when first introduced.

I asked Murphy why he was attacking Charlotte when he knew it distressed his family and made them angry with him. He replied that everyone thought Charlotte was beautiful and he wasn't beautiful anymore because his hair was falling out, so he was jealous. Murphy also told me the other dogs had much nicer dishes to eat from.

When I told Pam what Murphy was saying, she started crying. She told me she didn't think it made any difference what dish a dog ate from and was amazed that Murphy perceived the difference between the plain plastic bowl he ate from, and the other dogs' special stainless steel dog dishes. She hadn't realized that such a thing could matter to dogs or be interpreted by them as a sign of preferential treatment and favoritism.

I told Pam all of Murphy's undesirable behavior stemmed from his need for attention from his family, attention he felt he was no longer getting since the introduction of Charlotte to the household. The family was naturally cross with him for attacking Charlotte, not realizing that Murphy was so unhappy that it was the only way he knew to let his family and the other dogs know how he was feeling. He was getting his family's attention, even if it was the wrong kind of attention. Murphy was crying out to be loved.

Pam also had to put Murphy into a room by himself so he couldn't attack the other dogs, which only added to Murphy's distress because he felt very lonely and upset being shut away from his beloved family. I told Pam that instead of shutting Murphy away all the time, it should be used as a punishment when he attacked Charlotte. I instructed her to say very firmly to him, "No! You don't do that to Charlotte," and then put him in a room alone for about ten minutes every time he attacked, so he would realize the undesirable confinement was the direct result of his undesirable behavior, instead of believing the confinement was his family's way of shutting him out because they didn't love him anymore.

The sadness and upset Murphy was transmitting to me was disturbing, particularly because I knew the dog's distress was caused by his family's misunderstanding of the situation. I reassured Pam that many pet owners would have responded the same way to such a situation and asked her what she wanted to do. Pam said she wanted to keep Murphy, that she loved him very much, and had only suggested giving him away because she didn't know what else to do. I told her that I would speak to the dog and convey her love, but that she had to make the changes I suggested if she expected Murphy to show any improvement. Pam agreed.

I spoke to Murphy and assured him that Pam and his family still loved him very much, and that there was no reason for him to attack Charlotte again because his people all loved him as well as they loved Charlotte. I told him I knew he would be a very good dog now, and that even though I understood how he had felt so very jealous, there was no need any longer for that sort of behavior.

Murphy then asked about his hair. Apparently he had been pumped so full of steroids in an effort to cure the inflammatory condition that had caused the hair loss that his fur would never grow back. I heard my angel guides saying that he should be on a diet of rice and fresh fish; then his hair would grow in again. I told Pam about the special diet, and reminded her to get Murphy a new stainless steel dish. I then told Murphy he was going to get his own special bowl like the other dogs had.

Pam called my studio a few days later to tell me that everything was much better. Murphy had his new dish, and lots of love and reassurance from his suddenly cognizant family. Everyone in the family was telling him how beautiful he was.

Pam also reported that Murphy was getting along much better with the other dogs. While Pam was on the phone, I tuned in to Murphy, and he transmitted to me a good happy feeling; then he telepathically sent me a picture of him sleeping together with the other dogs. I also picked up another of Pam's dogs who told me that Murphy was a nice dog again. I was very pleased that the dogs were again communicating with each other, and that Murphy and his companions were all living in harmony once more.

A few weeks later, Pam brought Murphy to see me, and he had grown back a full coat of hair and was once again quite a beautiful dog. I could feel the pride and happiness flowing from him. Murphy has reestablished an important role with his family, and regularly receives outward shows of love and affection from them. This was all he needed to correct both his behavioral and health problems.

Pam is still distraught over the pain her family's thoughtlessness caused Murphy, but it is common that we humans fail to realize that animals are such intelligent and sentient beings. Humans often don't give animals credit for their ability to understand.

As long as each pet feels special to its family, loved, and appreciated, there should be no insurmountable problems. If real trouble begins after the introduction of a new animal, assess the time leading up to the difficulty and more often than not, you will pinpoint the cause.

Whiskey

Sometimes though, a new animal can be just the right prescription to cure problems with a lonely, bored, or skittish animal. The mingling of the two personalities often creates a more pleasant and tolerable atmosphere for both the pet with the difficulties and for the family. The amusement and distraction provided by another animal can often get a neurotic animal's mind off his own problems and onto more agreeable occupations.

This was the case with my friend Carol. She came to see me about her cat, Whiskey, who had taken to hiding under the bed all day long. No matter what enticement Carol presented, Whiskey would not come out from under the bed in her bedroom upstairs. When I started to speak with him, I discovered the first floor of Whiskey's house had taken in several feet of water during a devastating flood. The family was forced to climb to the upper floor to escape the water, and they were caught there until the water subsided. The rising waters, stormy weather, and his family's upset had terrified the poor cat.

After the disaster, the entire family had to live upstairs while the first floor was being repaired from the ravages of the flood. The commotion of strange workmen trooping in and out of the house all day, combined with the fearsome noise of their power tools, had just about collapsed Whiskey's nervous system. Carol told me he suddenly disappeared under the bed one day, and now he wouldn't come out, no matter what enticements she offered.

Through no one's fault, poor Whiskey had suffered so many terrible experiences he could not cope with what had happened. Whiskey had experienced so much trauma that he no longer wanted to come out from under the bed, the only place, except for a nice, dark closet, where he felt safe. But sitting alone under the bed, Whiskey had too much time to think about his troubles, so I suggested to him the idea of a new kitten as a companion. I also asked Carol if she had thought of getting a companion for Whiskey. She said if it would help Whiskey, she would be in favor of the idea.

As we communicated, I realized Whiskey was a very chatty cat. He sent me lots of details about his owner's dress and appearance. He liked the idea of having another cat around and gave his approval.

The arrival of the new kitten was planned in detail with Carol, to make sure that Whiskey felt included in all the preparations. I warned him that the kitten was likely to be nervous after leaving its mother and might hiss a bit. But I assured Whiskey that if he took good care of the kitten they would become

friends, and the friendship and amusement the kitten could provide would help take Whiskey's mind off his fear of another
flood.

As we had hoped, the two cats did become friends, and once
the curious little Samuel began to venture downstairs, Whiskey
could not help but follow. This was a great breakthrough. By the
end of the month, Carol reported that Whiskey and Samuel were
living in all the rooms of the house. Whiskey's old terrors about
being caught in another flood receded into memory.

In Whiskey's case, the addition of Samuel to the household
helped him overcome his fears and reclaim as his rightful territory
in all of his family's house.

No matter how difficult the situation, generally some resolution
can be found to the problems caused by new animals. Answers,
as always, lie in examining the changes in *human* conduct that
led to the changes in the pet's conduct. If your old pet truly
will not accept a newcomer, ask yourself why is it so important
to bring a new animal home? Do you really need another pet?
Can you provide for it properly, with nutritious food and good
veterinary care? Do you have enough time to give a new pet the
love and attention he needs? Or will the time you normally devote to the pets you already own have to be divided to accommodate all your animals, thereby knocking an established animal
from its accustomed perch in the pecking order?

If you want to ensure a happy result when you introduce a
new animal into your household, make sure the pets you already
have feel included in the planning stage. Tell them that a new
dog or cat is coming to live there and emphasize how much you
love and appreciate them, and how you think the new arrival
will be a wonderful addition to your family. Once the new pet

arrives, make sure the newcomer isn't allowed to displace the pets you already have. If you make a fuss over the newcomer, take the time to make a fuss over your old friends too to keep jealous feelings at bay. If you are wise and don't allow a new pet to change your relationship with your old pet, such additions can go smoothly, resulting in increased satisfaction and pleasure for all those involved. Trouble will surely result, though, if you don't plan ahead, and ignore your old pets in favor of a new darling.

Sometimes though, behavioral problems arise that are not due strictly to the introduction of a new animal. When owners inadvertently disrupt their pets' familiar environments, trouble can result. We discuss several examples in the next chapter.

CHAPTER SEVEN

Sonny's Proper Schedule

The Importance of Routine

I cannot emphasize too strongly to pet owners the importance of establishing a routine with their animal and sticking to it. With a reliable routine in place, pets are able to overcome some of the more common traumas, such as a change of house. To an animal which has no set routine, such a move is completely unsettling, because the only reliable thing in its life, its physical location, is suddenly taken away. An animal which still has its familiar bed, dish and toys, who is still enjoying its daily walk or romp with its owners, can come through such a transition with far fewer problems.

Though owners often come to see me about something specific such as a soiling or fighting problem, frequently I am able to trace the difficulty back to a change in their routine, something which has upset or frightened their pet, and resulted in the inappropriate behavior. Pets are so very like children. They need routine, discipline, and structure to stay on track, and when they do not get it, difficulties of one sort or another often arise. I often discover that a pet with significant behavior problems has had many different owners, or has suffered abuse. Many of these problems can be overcome with the establishment of a regular routine and lots of love. Once an animal has a routine he can trust and a relationship with his owner he can depend upon, he is likely to drop many undesirable habits or neurotic behaviors.

Your routine is one of the ways your animal tells time. Our pets know our daily routine and our weekend routine; that week-days have a different rhythm than weekends. They understand the concept of "day" and "night" as light and darkness.

If you go to work at the same time each day and arrive home around the same time each night, that is a routine your pet depends on. But work schedules vary and we all must work the occasional late night. It is important to let our pets know when we will be late, to keep them from worrying.

If you know you will be home late, try this exercise, because your pet will be expecting you and will be distressed if you don't show up on time. From your car or office, send a telepathic picture of darkness to tell your animal you are going to be home later than usual. Send the feeling of returning home later along with the words and the picture of darkness. Your message will reach your pet immediately, and he will know you'll be back later and not at your usual time. This will calm his fears about the break in the routine.

I have been consulted by people who were unsure how their pet knew exactly when to meet them even though their arrival time was different every day. One lady was especially puzzled. She stayed home with her children and was amazed by her dog barking to be let out into the garden a full ten minutes before her husband pulled up each night. Depending upon his workload, her husband's arrival times varied by as much as two hours, so she knew the time of day wasn't serving as the dog's cue. She wanted to know how their dog knew when the husband was on his way home.

The dog knew because the husband's mind energy was being transmitted telepathically as he commuted. I connected to the husband and discovered that while he was driving home, he sent out the feeling of pleasure he knew he would feel upon arriving home and finding his happy family waiting for him. His intelligent and very eager dog picked up this telepathic transmission immediately and barked to be let out into the garden so he could wait by the garage to greet his master and have his evening romp. It was clear to me that the husband's arrival home was an important part of this dog's daily routine. If something had disrupted his nightly jaunts to the garden, behavioral problems would have resulted.

As you go through your day, you are thinking about where you have to go and when you have to be there. Unbeknownst to you, all this information is transmitted telepathically to your animal, so they know you are about to leave the house, not only from the hustle and activity that precedes your departure, but also from the mental picture you have formed of going out to the car, starting the engine, and driving away to your destination. In the same way, when you are on your way home, you are transmitting images of your arrival, which your animal picks up. This is all part of your household routine.

If your animal is secure in his routine and knows he will be fed and walked regularly, played with, cared for and treated with great love and kindness, he is apt to experience few behavioral problems. An animal which has had no reliable care, endured thoughtless or cruel owners or many owners, and suffered through many changes of location, lives in a state of insecurity. There is nothing in his life he can rely on, so he tends to distrust humans and rely more upon himself. This often produces behavioral problems since an independent animal sees little benefit in cooperating with humans.

Sonny's Brass Horn

One of my cases involved a beautiful chestnut pleasure horse named Brass, so named because his burnished coat glowed like the brilliant metal. Gayle, his most recent owner, called me because Brass would not respond to his name or accept direction at all when she rode him. He preferred to follow his own lead and had taken Gayle on many wild and, occasionally, near-calamitous rides. His favorite trick was to gallop full speed under low-hanging branches. Gayle had a hard time trying to stay in the saddle. When he was behaving, however, he was a joy to ride, Gayle told me, with a satin-smooth gait like a rocking horse.

If Gayle hadn't been a particularly capable and courageous rider, she might have suffered serious injury. As we soon discovered, Brass, though still a stallion, was not an uncontrollable horse, merely a headstrong one. He wasn't trying to hurt Gayle, just gain control over a situation that was confusing and worrisome to him. Gayle was hoping I could find out why Brass behaved as he did and instill a bit more cooperative spirit in the horse. She loved him dearly and wanted to be able to trust him implicitly.

When I connected telepathically with Brass, he informed me immediately and with great indignation that he would not respond to the name Brass because that was not his name at all——his name was Sonny, very much like my own nickname. After I told him "Sunny" was my name too he seemed to warm a bit. But this was where the initial confusion came in. His first owner had named him Sonny's Brass Horn and called him "Sonny," and he couldn't understand why his subsequent owners, and there had been many, insisted upon calling him "Brass." He was adamant about this; "Sonny" was the only name he would answer to.

Then he told me he was very sorry about hurting Gayle's leg. When I told her this she was surprised because the injury had happened more than two years before when Sonny had panicked and jumped going over a creek, accidentally knocking Gayle over and landing on her left leg.

Gayle asked me to reassure Sonny that she knew it was an accident, which greatly relieved the stallion. Sonny then told me his life had been a series of changes, going from one owner to the next and suffering cruel treatment at the hands of many. He told me one of his owners beat him with a stick, causing him to fall to his knees and injure his right leg, which hurt him still. He had been very frightened. He was trying to do what the man wanted him to do, but couldn't understand what was required of him because the man was so angry all the time. Sonny also told me he'd been tied up in a pen and beaten across the forehead and back, which fortunately did not cause him permanent physical injury. But the abuse had left psychological scars.

This saddened me greatly. I have found through working with horses that they often suffer horrendous abuse at the hands of their trainers or handlers, beatings so severe it would kill a smaller animal. Is it any wonder that an animal which has been so badly abused would then turn against humans?

Because horses are such large animals, they are capable of inflicting serious injury on humans. Trainers should keep this in mind before they raise their hand to strike a horse. A horse may tolerate such mistreatment for a short time, but when it decides it has had enough, the results can be quite deadly.

Though Gayle was a kind and loving person who handled

Sonny gently, in her horse's experience humans were not to be trusted. Gayle was the first human he'd had contact with who hadn't abused him. He had been with Gayle more than two years and made her unhappy on more than one occasion, yet she had never resorted to striking him. He wanted to know if he could continue to rely on her kindness, and I assured him he could.

Sonny was also tired of all the moves and disruptions in his life. He wanted a steady routine and had taken it upon himself to provide one. He did not feel he could rely on anything or anyone, not even the exceedingly patient and good-hearted Gayle, who treated Sonny with the only love and kindness he had ever known.

After talking to Sonny for a while, I understood his behavioral problems were a direct result of the lack of routine in his life, combined with all the abuse. Mistreatment and constant change in his routine had made Sonny fearful, rebellious and not very willing to tolerate instruction from a human.

Sonny told me he loved Gayle very much, but they had been through a hard time together. He was afraid she was going to get rid of him, and he would have to start all over with a new owner. He didn't want that to happen, because he loved Gayle very much and thrived on all the attention Gayle showered upon him. He also liked having his own pasture, where he could run to his heart's content.

When I explained this to Gayle, she confirmed her horse had a difficult past. At one time she had considered selling Sonny, but now was determined to work with him until he learned what was required. When I told Gayle how Sonny had been cruelly beaten so many times, she started to cry. She had no idea he had been so badly abused. She promised to start addressing Brass by his preferred name of Sonny, and told me she was beginning to understand why he was so stubborn and willful, and so very skittish whenever a man approached him. In Sonny's experience, the appearance of a man meant a beating would soon follow.

After a time, Sonny had gotten used to Gayle's husband, Phil, who was as kind as Gayle. He allowed Phil to approach him in the stall or pasture without bolting. But all other men who came to work with Sonny, even if they were gentle, sent the stallion into a nervous state.

Sonny told me Phil was very worried Gayle would be seriously injured in a fall because of all the wild rides he had been giving her. He'd overheard Phil urging Gayle to sell him. I told this to Gayle and she said that Phil was indeed worried because of the ongoing problems with Sonny, but Gayle was determined to keep her horse and work through them. She wasn't worried about being hurt, because she knew the big stallion meant her no harm.

After speaking with Gayle, I assured Sonny he had a permanent home with her. He would not be moved again. I picked up a distinct love between Gayle and her horse, and knew he wanted to please her, so I told Sonny he must listen to Gayle, and do what she asked him to do. I reminded him of the love Gayle showed him daily, and the kind and thoughtful care she provided and would continue to provide for him. He knew Gayle would not harm him in any way, and I told him he could trust that feeling and trust Gayle. But he had to mend his ways and take care of Gayle when she rode him.

Gayle had said she was particularly worried about Sonny's tendency to get out of control when they were in the forest. He ran full speed after other horses in the woods with little regard for Gayle's safety. He sent me many pictures of Gayle falling off his back and she confirmed it happened more frequently than she liked, though it wasn't always Sonny's fault. He then told me he always waited for Gayle after she fell. Gayle confirmed this and said she considered it quite a bonus. Otherwise, she would have been in for many long walks after taking a spill in the middle of nowhere.

Interestingly, when I tried to talk to Sonny about the importance of Gayle's safety, he moved away from the fence and started eating grass, the picture of indifferent nonchalance. I knew immediately that he didn't want to hear this. He thought the chases in the forest were a game and great fun. He loved stretching his legs and running full-speed to see if he could pass up the other horses. He hadn't really been aware of Gayle on his back, hanging on to her wildly charging steed for her very life.

When I told Sonny his reckless behavior was a big problem for Gayle and that he had to be responsible for her safety when she was riding him, he moved back to the fence and started listening again. I told him he must pretend that he and Gayle were one and, therefore, had to move together. He couldn't go running off wildly into the woods anymore, endangering Gayle with his high-spirited play.

I also explained to Gayle that she could help the problem by putting herself inside of Sonny's body and feeling herself to be a horse, with her arms as his front legs and her own legs as his back legs. This way she could telepathically transmit the behavior she expected of him. If she wanted him to go slowly, she should imagine her own limbs moving slowly in a smooth, steady gait, and transmit that picture and feeling to Sonny. If she wanted him to halt, she should transmit that telepathically and Sonny would pick it up in his energy body and understand it much more quickly than any spoken command. If she could imagine herself to be one with the horse, the same as I had instructed Sonny, then they would learn to work together beautifully.

Gayle called the next day to say she'd had an interesting

canter with Sonny that morning. She said his gait was slower and choppy, almost as if he was trying very hard to rein himself in and provide her with a safe ride. I told her that we would keep working with him to let him know what she wanted, and that she would have the horse of her dreams by the time we were finished.

When next I visited, I discovered a distinct pride in Sonny. He told me he was a beautiful horse, which he was, and that he was a good jumper and could run very fast. That love of speed was the very thing which was worrying Gayle, so I told Sonny he could run as fast as he liked when Gayle was not on his back, but that whenever she was in the saddle, he had to keep his speed down and listen to Gayle. He said he would try his best to do this, because he loved Gayle and Phil, and wanted to please them. He was intelligent enough to realize the connection between his inappropriate behavior and Phil's fears for Gayle's safety and was determined to do his part to keep Gayle safe on his back.

Though Sonny is still difficult at times, Gayle reports his behavior and responsiveness is steadily improving. She has learned she cannot expose Sonny to unfamiliar men because it stirs bad memories, which in turn, trigger bouts of inappropriate behavior in the horse. She is careful to maintain Sonny's daily routine and not throw him any curves, because his checkered past has left him with little ability to cope with unfamiliar situations, which he always interprets as threatening.

The establishment of a reliable routine has had a most beneficial effect in this situation. Whenever I communicate with Sonny, I find he is becoming more relaxed and secure in the permanence of his home with Gayle and Phil. Gayle is concentrating on developing her ability to communicate telepathically with Sonny, which pleases him immensely. Sonny and Gayle have developed an even deeper and more spiritual bond as a result of their telepathic communication.

Topaz

My client Sylvia called me from New York because she was having a problem paper-training her red miniature poodle, Topaz. Sylvia lived in an apartment in Manhattan. She had suffered through a year-long period of ill health, during which time she had mostly been confined to bed and hadn't been able to take Topaz out. She had been trying to teach him to relieve himself on papers in a tiled bathroom, where any spillover would be easy to clean up. But Topaz kept going in the hallway, which annoyed Sylvia's housemate, David, to no end. David was kindhearted and had been trying to help Sylvia with the training, but they were not getting consistent results.

When I connected with Topaz, I discovered a very chatty, sociable dog, a real personality. I soon found the source of his confusion was the change in his routine. Before Sylvia became ill, he had been taken outside for walks, and encouraged to relieve himself there. After Sylvia could no longer take him out, Topaz couldn't understand what was required of him.

Topaz mentioned to me that he was a "star." I asked what he meant and he told me he went with David to entertain sick people and shut-ins as a clown dog. That gave me an idea. I told Topaz that stars didn't make messes in the hallway; that they always went on the paper in the bathroom.

I relayed to Sylvia what I had told Topaz and she confirmed the dog had worked briefly with David. But the long hours away from her owner became difficult once Sylvia became ill. She decided to keep the dog home with her to relieve the monotony of her confinement. She loved the little dog dearly and his cheerful company took her mind off her illness. The only problem was with his paper training.

Topaz was proud he had been able to cheer Sylvia during her illness and wanted to do whatever he could to help her. He promised me he would go on the paper, and stop wetting in the hall. But he wasn't through talking, not at all. He told me he liked his new red collar much better than his old one and liked socializing when he went to the pet center, where Sylvia sent him so he could play with other dogs. He also mentioned that he wished Sylvia would put his scarf back on. Sylvia was astounded when I told her that, because he'd only worn the scarf once, almost six months before. Still, Topaz remembered the scarf and felt it made him look very beautiful. Sylvia laughed and told me she would have to initiate a search for the scarf since she couldn't quite remember where she'd put it.

Then Topaz bragged that his mommy took him to the "beauty parlor" all the time and that made him even more beautiful than he already was. When I told this to Sylvia she laughed again, and confirmed that Topaz indeed enjoyed his regular visits to the groomer, where they doted on the charismatic little dog.

The next week, Sylvia reported that Topaz had started going on the paper immediately after I had talked to him, never missing. David couldn't believe it; he had tried everything he knew to train Topaz, and here, after one conversation, the little dog finally understood what was required and had started doing it perfectly. But I cautioned Sylvia that it was important to keep up the routine with Topaz, praising him every time he went on the paper.

Things went well until Sylvia went to her summer home in North Carolina. The change in routine and location threw Topaz off and he started having accidents again. Sylvia called, and I asked her about her new schedule. She told me that in North

Carolina, she expected Topaz to go outside the house, which had a large garden. This was completely different from what was required of him at home in Manhattan. The confusion had caused the same old problem we had solved in New York to resurface.

I explained to Sylvia that everything was brand-new for Topaz in North Carolina. Fortunately, she had recovered her health and was able to take Topaz outside, but Topaz had not yet made the connection between going outside and relieving himself. Sylvia was frustrated because he often relieved himself inside as soon as he returned from a walk. Of course he did, because that was the routine he was used to.

I told Sylvia to try and connect to Topaz telepathically whenever they went outside, and to send him the physical feelings and urgency of having to go to the bathroom so that he could understand what she wanted. I also communicated with him and explained that as this house had a lovely garden, he could relieve himself outside.

At first, we didn't have much success and Sylvia called me back, complaining that she walked Topaz three times a day but he always had an indoor accident right after his walk. When I connected to Topaz, I got a picture of a "walk" that was very fast indeed, perhaps no more than three minutes, and certainly not long enough for a dog who is not sure what to do. Don't forget that dogs like to sniff several dozen spots before deciding where to go, and this can be quite time-consuming even without the added element of Topaz's confusion. I told Sylvia she had to walk Topaz for at least twenty minutes each time, to give him a chance to understand what she wanted and to perform accordingly. I told her to use voice commands, and transmit feelings of urgency telepathically to Topaz, so he would get the idea of relieving himself in the garden before he went back inside the house.

This seemed to do the trick and Topaz soon understood that the change in his location had resulted in a change in what was required of him. He stopped soiling indoors. I cautioned Sylvia there was a slight chance she might undergo another period of difficulty once she returned to Manhattan. It was my feeling though, that Topaz had the hang of what was expected of him in New York and would not have a problem readjusting to that routine.

Though her business often requires that she be in New York, I wish Sylvia could stay in North Carolina, because Topaz has told me he loves it there. He enjoys the romps in the lovely garden and being able to watch the garden through the windows of the house when he is inside with Sylvia.

The only problem now is that telepathic communication has changed Topaz's whole personality. He has asked me why Sylvia can't talk to him the same way I can. I've told him that she can and that she is working very hard to learn how to do it. Sylvia has told me Topaz now expects to talk; that he literally starts "talking" whenever she starts speaking and expects to be understood. She can see it in his face. However, much like Sonny, when the topic turns to a problematic area, Topaz is not nearly so interested in the conversation.

Larkspur

I had a very sad case with a cat named Larkspur. His owners consulted me because he was having accidents all over the house. At first I thought it was a typical litter box problem, but when I connected telepathically to the cat, I discovered his owners were always leaving him unexpectedly for long periods of time while they traveled. Though they had Larkspur since he was a kitten, they had never bothered to establish a routine with him, and the poor cat never knew what was going to happen from one day to the next. Just as some parents don't tell their children what is happening even if it impacts them dramatically, so too did Larkspur's owners fail to inform him of the upcoming changes in his environment. Because of this, he lived in a state of distress.

Once, when the couple left the country, Larkspur was sent to live with the man's mother for three months, an arrangement the cat liked because the woman was very kind to him and paid him a lot of attention. During that time, Larkspur didn't have a single accident.

But for the next trip, the couple decided to put Larkspur with the man's sister for six months. The sister was far less patient with animals than her mother had been, especially after Larkspur started having accidents. She raised her voice to the cat and even struck him. Though I could fully understand her desire to maintain a clean house, free from the smell and stains that accompany pet accidents, I don't agree with her technique. The angrier she got, the more frightened and confused Larkspur became.

Though I tried to explain it to them, Larkspur's owners couldn't see the connection between their erratic schedule and their cat's accidents. They absolutely did not understand the importance of establishing a good routine to help their cat behave as they expected. Larkspur was completely unsure of their expectations of him. Because he didn't have one certain place to go to the bathroom, he became confused and started relieving himself wherever he happened to be at the moment.

When I connected to Larkspur telepathically, I discovered there was also an element of anger in his behavior. His life was a series of scenes—his family packing and leaving him again and again—and it distressed him terribly. The only way he knew to let them know how unhappy he was and that he didn't want his family to leave him again was to make a mess in the house.

When I explained this to the owners, they said they had to travel because their business required it. I can certainly understand how, in certain lines of work or if a couple is retired, this may be true. But my immediate thought was, why have a pet then if you must travel so much that you cannot give it a proper home? Time and again, I find people acquire pets for reasons of their own, giving little or no thought to the needs of the animal.

Like children, animals need guidance, training, and companionship. They require a commitment of time and caring to thrive. Puppies are not born with an innate understanding that they must relieve themselves outside and not on your carpets. You must teach them what you expect, and show them where to go. Cats have a natural inclination to exercise their claws by scratching, and furniture fits that need quite nicely. You must gently teach them that furniture is not to be scratched, and provide them with a suitable alternative. Such training requires patience and compassion. If you love your furniture more than you love your pet, then don't have a pet.

The easiest way to avoid problems with your pet is to establish a reliable routine in the beginning and stick with it. Don't constantly change the rules or your expectations, because your pet cannot keep up with such inconsistency.

All animals need open and regular displays of your affection. It is important that they feel a valued part of their human family. They also need to know when their routine is going to change; when you will be gone and for how long; when a new pet is coming in; or when you plan to move. It may sound silly for me to say you must discuss these things with your pet, but taking the time to do so can truly save you much difficulty down the road.

If you do have to alter the routine, remember that all animals are different. If your pets have trouble adapting to the requirements of a new environment, just be patient with them until you can establish a new routine. The establishment of such routines early on with your pet will make for a mutually rewarding and satisfying relationship. Pets want to please us but before they can do so, we have to communicate very clearly what we expect of them. Once we get our pets into a good routine, the rest is pure enjoyment.

WHILE establishing a regular routine with your pet is important, it is just as important to select an animal that suits your lifestyle. Choosing a pet whose size and physical requirements closely match your home environment and daily schedule can head off many problems. In the next chapter, I will discuss what it takes to be a responsible pet parent, covering everything from the selection of a pet to proper veterinary care to preparing for an emergency situation.

CHAPTER EIGHT

For the Love of Animals

How to Be a Responsible Pet Parent

*T*here are some people who think of animals as commodities that they buy and own just like a car or house or television set. Nothing could be further from the truth. Like a child, a companion animal is a gift from the universe that relies upon you for food, shelter and comfort, and in return, gives you unconditional love.

While most people do try to take good care of their pets, some keep their animals under shocking conditions. Whether from ignorance or indifference, this sort of maltreatment breaks my heart. In this chapter I will cover the principal responsibilities of being a good pet parent, and offer suggestions to make your pet's life as comfortable and enjoyable as possible.

Pet Selection

There are many different sizes and breeds of domestic animals. When you decide you would like an animal companion in your life, there are many things you must take into consideration.

First, what sort of space do you have available? If you live in a 800-square-foot condominium and have no yard, it would be cruel to select a large dog like a Great Dane for your companion because you can never meet his needs for exercise and play in such a small space unless you are prepared to walk him several miles every day. Better to select a small dog like a Chihuahua or Yorkie who would be more than happy in a cozy little space. When selecting a pet, you also must take into account the animal's natural habitat. If a dog has been bred to withstand extremely cold temperatures like an Akita or Husky, and you live in a region with high heat and humidity, you must take special steps to ensure the dog's comfort. Have their coats shaved down and keep them in air-conditioning. Do not leave them outside! Walk them early in the morning and in the cooler temperatures of the early evening, never at midday.

Dogs with heavy coats suffer tremendously when subjected to summer heat, so it's best not to select such a breed if you live in the deep South or the desert, or any place where temperatures are higher than average. By the same token, if you live in a climate that is very cold with lots of ice and snow, it would not be wise to pick a dog that has a light, thin coat like a Greyhound or Ridgeback bred for warm climates.

Don't insist on having a named breed if you want a dog or cat. There are thousands of mixed-breed puppies and kittens that need homes in our animal shelters. Mixed breeds make wonderful and loving companions, for nature has made hybrids strong in both body and spirit. In fact, some pure breeds are suffering woes as a consequence of generations of reckless and shortsighted breeding practices. Bulldogs, Mastiffs, Golden Retrievers and even little Dachshunds can develop a terribly painful and crippling disease known as hip dysplasia when breeders are not careful about watching which lines they are mixing.

Now you should consider what age pet to adopt. If you have lots of time to spend training an animal, you may well desire a puppy or kitten. If your time is constricted or you feel you don't have the patience or the resources to properly train your pet, you should consider getting an older animal that has already been house-trained and knows how to respond to simple commands such as, "sit" or "stay." If you have very small children, I don't recommend getting a puppy or kitten. Human babies and animal babies are rarely a good mix, because each can hurt the other without meaning to. Toddlers can squeeze and hit and pull tails, while puppies and kittens can nip and scratch. Find a breed that is good with children. Research before you bring the animal into the home as some breeds have more easygoing temperaments, which make them more suitable for homes with small children.

Next, consider whether or not anyone in your home suffers from pet-related allergies. If they do, it would be wise to limit your selection to animals without fur like birds, fish or reptiles like iguanas, as they generally do not trigger allergic reactions in sensitive individuals. If you absolutely must have a dog, select a short-haired breed that doesn't shed like the Ridgeback and that should minimize allergy problems.

Finally, you have to decide how many animals you want to adopt. Take into consideration the size of your living quarters and the amount of time you have to spend with your animal. If you spend all day at work, then your pet would dearly appreciate another animal as a companion, but it is always best to adopt them together. If you are adopting kittens from a shelter and they are siblings, always take at least two (two are just as easy as one). They have become used to depending upon each other and it is traumatic to separate them. They will cry for each other pitiably; you can head off potential problems by taking two kittens home instead of just one, not to mention that two kittens are much more fun to watch than one and are just as easy to care for.

Food

Unfortunately, much of the food that is commercially available for domestic pets is filled with additives and cheap ingredients that can be detrimental to your pet's health. On March 11, 1997, the *New York Times* published an investigative article revealing that parts from diseased animals are used in the manufacture of some types of cat and dog food, and it is in this fashion that disease can be spread.

Pets require good nutrition to thrive and remain healthy. The easiest way to ensure the health of your pets is to cook for them yourself. You can steam a pound of brown rice along with sliced garlic, green peas and carrots as a good nutritious base. Then mix it with diced roasted chicken. Your dogs will gobble down this delicious meal time after time. This recipe has the added advantage of acting as a natural flea repellent because eating garlic is a blood purifier and causes a subtle change in a dog's body odor that fleas don't like.

Cats require more protein than dogs do. In fact, if a cat is fed food formulated for a dog long enough, it can actually go blind from a lack of protein. Sadly, many of our ocean fish are contaminated with mercury and other heavy metal, but I still do give my cats raw meat, fresh fish, grains and eggs.

Animals love treats, but not all treats are created equal. Select those made from wholesome, natural ingredients. Be careful in your selection of brand and avoid those that contain cheap fillers and chemical preservatives. Use treats such as dog biscuits to help train your animal and to reward him for good behavior. Be careful not to feed too many or else you will disrupt your pet's feeding schedule and may even cause an unhealthy weight gain.

Many municipal water supplies are contaminated with heavy metals like lead or contain additives like fluoride that can be detrimental to your animal's health. Always give your animal filtered or bottled water to drink and never use tap water if you can avoid it. Change the water daily to keep it fresh, particularly in hot weather. Water that has been sitting out for several days develops a stale, flat taste, and most pets will not drink it. Once a week, clean the water dish thoroughly with salt and rinse it thoroughly to prevent the formation of algae in the bowl. If you have many animals, you may wish to invest in a pet drinking fountain, which keeps a continuous supply of fresh, filtered water circulating through a drinking basin.

It is unfortunate that many veterinary practices offer and promote a very selective range of brand-name pet foods and very rarely advise or comment on the benefits of home pet food preparation as a healthier and cheaper alternative, which can be further improved by the judicious addition of selected nutrients. For information about preparing your pet's diet yourself, I recommend a wonderful book called, *The Nature of Animal Healing*, by Martin Goldstein, D.V.M., published by Alfred M. Knopf.

Toys

It is part of animals' nature's to play, so you should provide appropriate toys. Animals that are bored because they are lonely and have nothing to amuse themselves with can develop behavioral problems like chewing and barking. Better to head the problem off before it develops.

Dogs naturally like to chew, so be sure you provide plenty

of chewable objects or else they'll find your best shoes or the corner of a convenient table and gnaw away. There are many different brands of chews on the market, but not all are safe. Tragically, several dogs lost their lives during the past few years due to intestinal obstructions caused by broken pieces of hard plastic from a particular nationally known brand of chew bone (it has since been removed from the market).

Balls and Frisbees are another favorite dog toy because dogs love to retrieve items that have been thrown. Just be sure the ball is large enough to prevent your dog from swallowing it and made of a sturdy material that will stand up to chewing. If you're out with your dog and find that you have forgotten its toys, you can always pick up a sturdy stick for a rousing game of pitch and fetch.

Dogs also like to play tug-o-war. There are several rope toys designed for this very game; again select one that is an appropriate size for your dog. Dogs also love stuffed animals; in fact, they can be quite possessive and protective of them. Just be sure to treat your pets equally; if you buy a toy or a treat for one, make sure you do the same for all of them, or problems of jealousy may arise that can lead to fighting. Also watch for problems with bones. You may find that dogs that never fight at any other time may fight over bones, so always pick up all the bones from the floor before you go out. Some of my worst cases of dogs fighting while their human companions are out happened because the dogs were left alone with bones and got into a tussle over them. In one case, a dog lost an eye in this sort of fight, so be very careful.

Cat toys are another matter altogether. They usually feature lots of action, maybe even a bell or whistle, and probably contain catnip to spark your cat's interest. Cats are particularly fond of small catnip mice they can carry around in their mouths like a baby. Feathers attached to a stick with elastic strings that they can chase through the air are another popular cat toy. Cats also love to crouch and leap and hide and pretend they are jungle tigers. There are several excellent cat trees available that feature a variety of hiding holes and climbing poles. Cats love them.

As discussed in chapter 4 don't forget to provide your cat with a suitable scratching post. It must be of sufficient height to allow your cat to stretch from end to end when its claws are sunk into its top. And it must be strong and sturdy enough to stand up to your cat's weight. If it tips over, your cat will likely become frightened and will not use the post again after that.

Remember that each animal has its own unique personality. Don't be upset if your animal companion doesn't seem to be interested in a toy you have picked out. Many animals ask me what happened to their blue toy or their mouse. People often think if an animal does not play with a toy they should give it away, or put the toy where the animal can no longer see it. Some animals just enjoy looking at their toys even though they don't play with them. Just because they don't play with a particular toy doesn't mean they don't like it. Pets get upset when you give them a present and then take it away.

The important thing is to find something your pet enjoys and play with them frequently. Pets regularly need your undivided attention. Many behavior problems stem from you not playing with your pets often enough or spending enough time talking with them, down on your knees and nose-to-nose. A regular playtime accomplishes several things. It provides healthy exercise for your pet and releases pent-up energy for both of you. It makes your pet feel loved and valued when you spend quality time playing with it. And finally, playtime builds and seals the bond of love and mutual appreciation between you and your animal companion.

Bedding

Your animal companion needs a comfortable place to call his own where he can lie down and sleep undisturbed each night. Beautiful dog and cat beds are available in a variety of colors, sizes and styles. Of course, most of us just have our pets sleep in our own beds. Just be sure there is enough room for everyone! My seven dogs and cats take up an enormous amount of room in my bed!

My dogs and cats share my bed as I know many of your pets do. However, some dogs and cats prefer to have their own bed as well as sharing ours. My home is animal friendly and is designed around my furry companions with tiled floors and no carpets downstairs. I put white cotton bed throws over my sofas so they always look fresh and chic. I wash them in very hot water with nonchlorine bleach.

I have Rachel Ashwell Shabby Chic chairs with loose white covers, which are easy to take off and wash. I find white is a fab color. People often say to me, "White shows the dirt." My reply is that I want to see the dirt, not hide it.

My bed is always covered with a giant Mattisse cotton cover and my dogs and cats can go on my bed whenever they like. The cover is very easy to wash. I also have cushioned wicker beds on the floor throughout the house and my cats love these beds.

You may also wish to keep small blankets or towels to cover your furniture so that your pet may jump up and relax without fear of soiling or staining. It is much easier to throw a blanket into the wash than to try and remove a stain from an expensive sofa. To them, a sofa or chair in their house is a natural part of their environment and it's very confusing when they are allowed on some chairs or furniture some of the time but not all the time. Either allow your pets on the furniture all the time or keep them off. They do not think like humans and cannot understand conflicting directions regarding furniture. Better to cover all your furniture and keep it clean by frequently washing the covers. Then, when company comes, all you have to do is remove and fold the covers and your lovely furniture will be ready to greet guests. Even easier is to select decorative washable covers that match the color of your furniture, so that your home is always ready to welcome a visitor.

If you have a small caged pet like a hamster or a lizard, it is essential that you change the bedding every few days. A dirty cage can result in a whole host of problems for small animals, including an increased incidence of infection, loss of appetite and behavioral changes like pacing or incessant chewing. Even if the pet belongs to your child, it is your responsibility as the adult in the house to make sure the pet's living conditions are optimal. Children often forget their chores, so before you allow a pet into your home, know that your child might not be responsible about the pet's daily care. If you leave it up to the child, the animal will suffer. We choose to have our pets come into our homes, and we are obligated by that choice to do the very best we can by them.

Exercise

Just like humans, animals must exercise regularly to maintain strong and healthy bodies. If you have a dog, one good long walk a day of perhaps thirty minutes will allow your dog to run, explore, sniff and examine to its heart's content.

I have frequently been called to help locate lost dogs that have been confined to a narrow half block or block radius from their homes on their walks. While some dogs can pick up a familiar scent to find their way home, other dogs become frightened and confused and often start running without stopping to smell for clues. When they stop running they are unable to locate anything that is familiar to them and they are completely lost and disoriented.

Once these poor animals get lost they are truly lost, because they don't recognize any familiar landmarks once they get more than a block from home. Start today taking your dog on far-ranging walks to acquaint him with the whole of your neighborhood and its natural boundaries such as large streets, creeks, fences, etc. This will benefit not only his health but also yours, and in the event that your pet does get lost, offer a much greater likelihood that he will find his way home using familiar landmarks along the way.

Many people believe that when they have a yard or acreage it is not necessary to walk with their dogs, but that is not true. It is very important for you to walk with your dogs every day. Imagine how you would feel cooped up in the yard all day. Dogs love to share a walk with their human companions and daily walking not only provides excellent exercise for both human and dog, it gives your pet a sense of comfort and familiarity with the neighborhood surrounding their homes. Dogs that do happen to get out of their yards will know how to find their way back if they already know the neighborhood landmarks firsthand.

Dogs love to sniff and pick up messages from other dogs' scents along the way; they also like to leave messages of their own for other canines to investigate. So give them plenty of time to sniff out the messages left by other dogs. It's rather like when you are reading a letter from a friend. Just as you may reread your favorite parts over and over again, dogs may like to linger for quite a while at a particularly intriguing spot. If you pull them away too quickly without giving them time to investigate

all the scents along your path, it's just as if someone had yanked
your friend's letter from your hands before you had time to finish
reading it. You would be upset by such a circumstance, so give
your dogs time to finish reading their "letters" during their daily
walks.

A word of warning about letting your dogs out on acreage
without supervision: many people who live in the country have
had dogs lost or stolen when they've left them out alone. Many
of my clients have found that their dogs have not returned home
after they let them out to sun alone or to roam with other dogs
in the woods or surrounding countryside. When dogs are out in
such circumstances, pack instincts may take over and the pack
may well lead your beloved pet deeper and deeper into the wild.
Better to fence off a portion of your land so that your dogs may
be kept safe and close to your home.

I had one very sad case with a young man Brian, who loved
his two dogs passionately. He lived on ten wooded acres. One
day his dogs did not return home after he had let them out to
run. He was puzzled because he had been letting them out daily
for five years with no problems. An animal-control officer who
saw the two dogs running shot them both and claimed he did so
because the dogs had attacked him. Brian knew this could not
be true as his dogs were very friendly and often met with his
neighbors on their runs. He was unable to bring a case against
the animal-control officer since the dogs had been incinerated as
soon as the officer returned to the pound, destroying any evi-
dence. After making further inquiries, Brian discovered this had
happened to many other people's pets in the vicinity and that
this officer had a habit of shooting dogs that were running loose
in their rural neighborhood. Brian's story is not the only sad
story of dogs being lost by their human parents after they were

allowed to run free without supervision. So keep your dogs safe; it is up to you.

For you singles out there, there have been studies proving that people who want to chat and socialize are five times more likely to approach someone walking a dog than someone just walking alone. Dogs are a natural icebreaker in social situations and dog lovers feel naturally drawn to someone who is walking a dog. So don't sit home moping another night. Get out the leash and take your best friend to the park. You may meet someone very special there!

Cats are more problematical. You cannot put a cat in a harness and expect it to cheerfully follow you about as a dog will. So offer plenty of opportunities inside your home for your cat to climb, jump and stretch. Just like dogs, cats love a good game of chase, but instead of chasing you or a Frisbee, cats like to chase stuffed toys that look like mice and birds. If you play chase and provide both good scratching and climbing surfaces, your cat should get all the exercise it needs.

If you have small animals like hamsters, it is essential that you provide exercise wheels for them. Without proper exercise, many animals may become sick and grow weak.

If you look upon your pet's requirements for regular exercise as an opportunity rather than a challenge, you may well find your own health improving along with that of your pet. If you are the sort who doesn't enjoy exercise, think how much more enjoyable your daily walk will be with the company of your animal companion. Together, the two of you can beat the battle of the bulge.

Cleanliness and Pest Control

All animals are subject to attack by pests such as fleas and ticks. Regular and thorough cleaning can go a long way toward eliminating these nuisance insects. Weekly washing of your pet's bedding and regular vacuuming of your floors and carpets will interrupt the insect's life cycle and keep new generations from hatching.

Consult with your veterinarian about the type of flea repellent he recommends. Don't use strong chemical insecticides as these poisons can have devastating consequences for your pet. In the past two years there have been a rash of cat deaths following the application of a commercial poison that destroyed their neurological systems. These poisons are cheap and readily available in discount department stores, but is it really worth risking your pet's life and well-being just to save a few dollars on pest control each month?

In warm climates, you must also take steps to protect your pet from heartworms, which are transmitted by mosquitoes. Once-a-month treatments are available that offer total heartworm protection, and some brands are combined with a flea and tick repellant as well. Your veterinarian can recommend the right formula and dosage for your pet. Be sure to have your pet tested for heartworms before giving the first dose as the treatment is somewhat different for animals that already have them in their systems.

Misbehavior

Behavioral problems of one sort or another are one of the most frequent reasons why people consult me about their animal companions. There is always a logical reason why the pet is behaving as it is, and it always relates back to something its human has said or done, or left unsaid or undone; that is generally the root of the problem.

Remember that animals are aware of everything we say and

even what we are thinking. They pick up our thoughts on the telepathic channel. So, if you are thinking of getting rid of an animal, this can produce enormous stress, which in turn, can lead to behavioral problems. You might be asking, "Well, if he knows I am thinking about giving him away because he is misbehaving, wouldn't that make him want to act better?" But animals' minds do not work in the same logical way that ours do. They act out their worry and fear in ways that may seem contrary to us, but it is their way of telling us they are distressed about something. It is up to us to work out what is causing the problem and remedy the situation.

My friend Elvia contacted me because her beautiful orange-winged Amazon parrot, Luna Balloona, had started picking out all her feathers. When I connected to the bird telepathically, I found she was distressed because she missed the green eucalyptus leaves that Elvia used to put in her cage. She missed this element from her natural environment; living without green leaves and trees around her made Luna unhappy.

Elvia was amazed when I told her what Luna had said. She told me that the tree she obtained these leaves from was by her mechanic's shop and that after the mechanic moved, she stopped getting the leaves, not realizing what an effect this would have on Luna. It so happened the tree was also very close to her vet's office, so the next time she went there, she stood on the hood of her car and pulled down an armful of branches for Luna to enjoy. When Elvia and her husband move to their summer residence, there are no eucalyptus leaves to be had, so once a month, she has a friend send her a big box of eucalyptus branches to keep Luna happy.

No matter what the animal's problem behavior—nipping, nervous barking, chewing, spraying, scratching, soiling—you can be assured that it has its origins in something a human has said or done. When I talk to dogs that are excessively nervous around people, I almost always find that they have been beaten or have experienced cruelty from a human in the past so they do not trust humans. It takes time, love and patience to restore trust in a dog that has been badly treated, but the joy you will experience in your loving bond with such a dog is well worth the investment of your time. I find that a housebroken animal that suddenly starts having accidents is usually upset by a change in routine; perhaps there's a new baby in the house or the family has moved or introduced a new pet. If you are sensitive to these changes and make sure to spend some extra time with your pet each day to reassure him of his importance, it will go a long way toward heading off potential problems.

If you would like to establish better communication with your pet, read through the chapter on telepathic language so that you will know how to better explain to your furry friend in a language that he understands exactly what you want from him.

Moving

One of the most stressful situations for pets (as well as humans) is moving. All their familiar and comfortable toys and furniture are suddenly whisked away and packed into trucks and boxes. There's an ongoing commotion of strange people coming and going and a general tenseness your animals can sense.

Of course, moving is a fact of life. Whether we are changing jobs, moving closer to relatives, retiring, or whatever the reason, there are going to be times in our lives when it is unavoidable. You can spare your pet a lot of misery and uncertainty by taking a few simple steps before you start the moving process.

When you know for certain that you will be moving, you can be sure that your pet knows it as well. Cats will not share your same confidence and enthusiasm, but dogs often enjoy a change and will be very happy as long as you are with them.

Spend a few quiet minutes with your pets explaining the move and describing the new house they will be going to. Reassure them that you love them and that they are a very important part of your life. Tell them that you will make sure the move goes as smoothly as possible for them.

Do not let their favorite toys and bedding be swept up willy-nilly in the excitement of the move. Make a moving kit in much the same way that you prepare an emergency kit for your animal. Include favorite toys, treats and bedding, and a recently worn item that has your scent on it to comfort your pet during the move. Make sure you get your pet's health records from your veterinarian so your new veterinarian can know its health history.

If you are just moving across town, transport your pet yourself but explain to him how he will experience the journey. If you are moving across country you will have to rely on an airline or some other shipping service to move your pet. You must prepare your pet for this journey by telling him in advance everything that will happen.

You have to use your imagination. Put yourself into your animal friend's body and try to experience the move as he would. If you have a cat, put a T-shirt with your scent on it inside the carrier, or see the pet carrier and feel yourself going into the carrier, sending calmness to your pet as you go. Explain that you are going to cover the crate to help them make the journey more comfortably. Hear the unfamiliar noises with your ears, the smell of the airport and feel the crate being transported. Become your cat or dog in that crate; put yourself into his body. Smell the tarmac with your nose, the journey through the airport. Hear the noises of the plane with your ears, feeling calmness all the while. If you remember to transmit a sense of calm to your pet during the actual move, he will pick up this feeling from you telepathically and it will ease his fears considerably. This will go a long way toward helping your pet successfully come through the trauma of a move.

Once you reach your new home, you must watch your pet carefully and keep him confined indoors for a number of weeks. More cats and dogs are lost during moves than at any other times. Cats particularly have a habit of running off from a new home and after one is lost, you occasionally hear of one showing up hundreds of miles away and months later, thin and bedraggled, at the doorstep of their old, familiar home. Walk your dog daily to familiarize him with the scents of his new neighborhood and keep your cats confined indoors for at least two weeks following the move to give them a chance to bond with their new surroundings.

Animals may be upset by a move because the scent of their new home is strange to them. You can help them with the transition by bringing a rug or blanket from the old house so that they have a familiar smell to comfort them. Don't wash it for a while. This helps them adjust to the scents in the new environment

While moving can be a traumatic experience, with a little bit of planning you can make sure that it goes as well as possible. By speaking the telepathic language your animal understands and experiencing what he will experience beforehand, the move will be much less traumatic for him.

Emergency Preparedness—Planning for Your Pets' Needs in a Time of Crisis

No one of us is immune from accidents or disaster. Emergencies can strike any time, anywhere, often with no warning. Some of you may well have a small family emergency kit prepared—extra batteries along with a short-wave radio, blankets, spare clothing, a few gallons of water and a few cans of food (and don't forget a can opener!). But have you thought of what your animal companions might need in such circumstances?

Hardly a day goes by that we don't read of some natural or man-made disaster—fires, floods, hurricanes, tornadoes, mud slides—and all too often, animals suffer needlessly from these events because their human companions failed to take their needs into account. And how often do we hear tragic stories of animals abandoned in the face of a fire or flood because their owners mistakenly believed the pet could "fend for itself?"

Our animal companions have an amazing capacity for many things, including being able to sense hours ahead of time when an earthquake or flood is coming, and minutes before a tornado ever shows up on radar. Cats and dogs alike will start howling and engaging in erratic behavior when they sense an impending event. They know something is about to happen because their small bodies are much more sensitive than ours are to the changes in the earth's magnetic field caused by geological shifts and changes in the atmosphere due to barometric and meteorological changes. When an electrical storm approaches, many animals can feel the static electricity in the air in their bodies and this causes them to become fearful and hide. Some animals seek out a way to ground themselves during electrical storms, so you might find them curled up next to plumbing pipes or porcelain toilets or tubs because this helps them discharge the uncomfortable buildup of static in their bodies.

Animals can smell smoke before we humans even wake up, alerting us of fire danger in time to save our lives. Every year I hear many cases where animals have saved their entire human families from a blaze. But as clever as they are, our domesticated animals cannot provide for themselves. That is our responsibility.

The very fact that we have domesticated our animal companions means that we have taken away some of their natural ability to survive on their own. They rely on us for everything. It is unconscionable to think that someone who purports to be an animal lover could abandon his or her pet in the face of a crisis, and yet, this sort of thing happens every day.

It's surprising just how many people do not think of their pets when an emergency strikes. It breaks my heart when I read of animals left behind during an evacuation, or lost because they were separated from their parents during the panic. I feel their terror and confusion; their overwhelming sadness that their human companions have abandoned them just when they need them the most. After every natural disaster, you read of hundreds of homeless animals wandering the streets, hungry, terrified and desperately searching for their families. But unless you have an emergency plan in place, your animal companion may well end up as one of these tragic statistics. And if you wait until the moment of crisis and then try to hurriedly put together an emergency kit, it will be difficult to think of everything your furry friend might require.

In order to make sure you are ready to evacuate with your pet and survive comfortably for several days in a shelter, you should make up an emergency kit to take care of your pets' needs during the crisis. Do it now, before an emergency strikes. Pick a quiet, calm time to put this vital kit together, a time when you are undistracted. It may save your pet's life.

Here are some simple tips to make sure your pet is well taken care of in the event you fall victim to an accident or disaster. Select a tote or some other bag large enough to accommodate everything your pet might need during an emergency, and then store this bag with all the supplies your animal requires inside the carrier you will use to transport your pet from the area of danger.

IDENTIFICATION

The very first thing you must do to prepare for a potential emergency is to determine a way to reliably identify your pet if the worst happens and you do become separated. If you own a dog or cat and they wear collars or harnesses, make sure their ID tags with their name and your name and contact information are securely attached. If you do not use collars or harnesses, consider the new microscopic ID tags that most veterinarians are now offering. The tag is actually a computer chip with a unique ID number that is read by a scanning device. The chip is so tiny that it can be easily embedded right below the surface of the pet's skin. After the injection, you register with a monitoring service, giving them all the information necessary to reliably establish your relationship with your pet. Should your pet be lost, the monitoring service checks its data banks to see if your pet's ID number has been reported. In the same fashion, people involved with pet rescues following a disaster know to scan recovered animals for the ID chips. All those pets with chips can be easily identified and returned quickly to their proper owners.

TRANSPORTATION

If you do receive an order to evacuate, explain to your animal companion that you will be leaving home for a few days, and tell him once again that he will be safe with you and that you have provided for all his needs during the emergency. Be sensitive to the fact that this is a time of great uncertainty for your furry friend. Talk to him gently to settle his fears and keep him informed about what is happening. This simple technique will go a long way to head off any problems that might develop as a result of the animal's fear of what is happening.

The safest way to carry an animal during an evacuation is in a carrying case specifically designed for its size and species. You should have a carrier for each of your pets. If you try to take a dog into a boat or out of a fire on a leash, he may panic and slip his leash and then be lost. And those of you who are cat owners know the impossibility of trying to carry a frightened feline in your arms. It's better to contain your animal companion entirely in a safe carrier of sufficient size to allow him to turn around and lie down. Carriers are also desirable because there are a number of shelters that will not allow animals that are not in carriers.

As part of your pre-crisis preparations, call the local emergency services providers in your area and inquire about their regulations for animals. Some shelters allow animals in carriers; others do not. For example, during a recent tropical storm in my area, none of the local Red Cross shelters would allow evacuated families to bring their pets into the shelter. If you find this to be the case, you must make arrangements with a local kennel or boarding facility ahead of time and evacuate early enough to have time to drop your pet off there before going to the emergency shelter. Ask your kennel if they will accept a standing reservation for your animals in case of emergency. If you wait until a storm or other emergency is upon you, you may find it impossible to find safe accommodations for your animal companions.

Never, under any circumstance whatsoever, should you leave your animal companions alone to fend for themselves in an emergency. Abandonment is traumatic for animals in any circumstance; when abandonment is accompanied by a natural disaster such as a fire and flood, the situation can be terrifying. Remember that your furry friends are your responsibility and they depend upon you to keep them safe and out of harm's way.

Try to keep your pet calm. Speak to him in a quiet and soothing tone of voice and hold him firmly but gently as you guide him into the carrier. (Please do remember to take out your tote bag of supplies before putting your pet into the carrier!) If the animal is so upset that he won't go into the carrier, try an old trick that horse trainers have used for more than a hundred years to remove panicked horses from burning buildings. Take a soft cloth or towel and cover your pet's eyes. Continue speaking in a soft voice and explain what is happening. Assure your animal friend that you will keep him safe and tell him that he can help you by going quietly into the carrier.

You may want to bring along a light blanket to keep the carrier covered, as being cut off from visual stimuli may help your pet to settle down quietly.

FOOD AND WATER

Keep a week's supply of your pet's favorite dry food in a plastic container stored inside the carrier. I say dry instead of wet because there are no facilities for individual dish washing in most shelters, and dry makes much less mess. Do this even if you regularly cook your pets' meals, because you will find very few emergency shelters will accommodate people trying to provide home cooking for their pets. Normally speaking, the sort of food served in crisis situations is not anything you would want to give your pet. Better to select a high-quality dry food and store the container inside the pet's carrier. Do remember to change out the food every month or so to keep it fresh. You wouldn't want to get to a shelter and find your dry pet food had gone stale or rancid.

Estimate how much water your pet drinks in the course of a

week and store that amount in the carrier along with the food. The gallon containers of bottled water are quite handy. I know that water is heavy to carry, but it is often quite difficult to secure drinkable water in the days immediately following a disaster, particularly in the case of a flood where the safety of the water supply may have been compromised by contaminants.

If space permits, you may also bring some of your furry friend's favorite toys and treats. Sometimes just a few minutes of playtime accompanied by the reward of a treat may be enough to settle your animal down by distracting them from the unfamiliar situation.

Toys and Other Comfort Items

If your pet is used to sleeping with you each night, you can be assured that won't likely be possible in a shelter situation. It is quite traumatic for an animal used to sleeping with its humans to suddenly be forced to sleep alone in its carrier.

You can help ease the situation by providing your animal with a T-shirt or some other item of clothing you have worn recently. Put this into the carrier with your pet and your scent will go a long way toward comforting him. In order for this to be effective, it is essential the item not be washed, as that will remove your scent and replace it with the chemical smell of washing powder, which most pets find offensive.

It may also be helpful to bring two or three of your pet's favorite toys. Pets can get bored just as easily as children do, and a toy or two may help them to pass the time. Familiar toys can be a great comfort in a strange situation. While it is understandable that a bored and frightened pet out of his normal environment may exhibit a few behavioral problems, we, as responsible pet parents, can do a lot to help them remain calm.

One final reminder: These last items are not things you can

prepare ahead and put in the kit, so I suggest you put a reminder to get an article of your clothing and a few toys for your pets on your final "to-do" checklist that you follow as you are preparing to leave your house. That way you will remember to include these important items in your pet's emergency preparedness kit.

While it is my wish that none of you would ever have to face an emergency situation, I do hope that you will take the time to make up an emergency preparedness kit for your pet. If the unthinkable does happen, at least you will have what you need to care for your animal companion close at hand.

Spaying and Neutering

Here is one of the most horrifying statistics I have ever read: The Humane Society of the United States estimates that five to six million dogs and cats are euthanized in shelters each year because there are no homes for them, and no money to feed and keep them indefinitely in the shelter. The simple way to turn this number around it to be a responsible pet parent, which means, ALWAYS spay or neuter your animal companion before it gets pregnant and has puppies or kittens.

According to SPAY USA, an unspayed female dog or cat and her unspayed offspring could produce an astonishing 67,000 babies in a six-year period. While that is a theoretical number that does not take into account how many might be spayed or neutered or how many succumbed to natural causes, the number still gives an idea of the scope of the problem. My advice here is simple: Be part of the solution and not part of the problem. Routine spaying and neutering can help reduce the pet population and also gives animals already waiting in shelters a better chance to find a loving home.

Breeding

On occasion people have told me that they would like their dog or cat to have a litter of puppies or kittens. They put their human emotions into their reasoning, telling me they do not want their animal companion to miss out on the experience of being a mother. When I speak to animals about this, however, they often tell me they do not want to have a litter of babies. It can be a frightening experience for them. Yes, some animals do look forward to motherhood, but many don't, so don't automatically assume that having puppies or kittens is best for your pet.

Declawing, Tail Docking and Other Unfortunate Practices

Sometimes people do things to their pets without stopping to think how it will make the animal feel. It breaks my heart when I see cats that have had their claws removed, or dogs with cropped ears and docked tails. Before you put your pet through these barbaric procedures, stop to consider exactly why you are doing it. Is it for fashion? For your convenience? To save your furniture? To make your pet match a show standard? Are any of these reasons sufficient to force your pet to endure such pain and suffering?

Please don't forget that any exposure to general anesthesia carries a risk of death or permanent disability for your pet. (You can minimize this by locating a vet who uses a special machine to monitor your pet's state of consciousness while anesthetized.) To voluntarily put yourself under the knife for a bit of surgical sprucing up is one thing; to do it to your helpless pet who depends upon you for its love and care is quite another.

All animals are beautiful just as they are. They do not need surgical "help" to become more attractive or to make their behavior more compliant. Surely it is long overdue to question the outmoded and time-encrusted prejudices behind these barbaric practices that mutilate animals soley for the pursuit of supposed aesthetic improvements. The idea that someone would subject their pet to the dangers of anesthesia and days of extreme pain and discomfort simply to match the animal's appearance to some concocted ideal is appalling.

Nor should we resort to surgical alternatives as a substitute for proper training. A bit of time and loving attention spent showing your cat where to scratch in the first few weeks he is in your home will pave the way for a lifetime of good behavior and rewarding companionship, as well as completely eliminate any damage associated with problem scratching.

What Is Declawing?

Feline onchyectomy or declawing is the surgical removal of a cat's claws, along with the nail bed and attached bones and tendons. The human equivalent would be to have the first digit of every finger on your hand amputated. If you can imagine what it might be like to have to go through life missing the ends of all your fingers, then perhaps you can start to understand why I am so opposed to declawing.

Some people think of a claw as the equivalent to a human fingernail but this is not exactly so. Unlike human nails that grow from a root bed just like a hair, a cat's claws actually grow from the bones of the paw and are attached to tendons that allow the cat to extend and retract the claw at will.

Declawing surgery is considered so painful that many pharmaceutical companies use it on laboratory cats to test the effectiveness of their various painkillers before they send them to market. And remember that cats react quite badly to most analgesic compounds, making it difficult for a veterinary surgeon to provide them any postoperative pain relief for this excruciating surgery.

Because a cat's body is designed to work with claws, amputating part of its paws to remove the claws drastically affects the animal, both physically and psychologically. When their claws are removed, cats lose their primary line of natural defense and they may become nervous biters as a result. Many groomers loath to handle declawed cats because of the frequency with which they bite. In addition, many cats undergo noticeable personality changes following declawing surgery. Some may become extremely aggressive and unpredictable in their behavior toward humans; others act traumatized and become timid and fearful. Neither outcome is desirable.

If declawing surgery is not performed properly, part of the claw may grow back, but in an unnatural position, such as sticking up from the top of the foot, which can cause a lifetime of misery and medical complications for the cat, including ongoing infections and drainage, not to mention horrendous pain. The surgery can also have a detrimental effect on a cat's balance and may lead to atrophy of the muscles of the shoulders, neck and back, as the cat's primary means of exercising them has been taken away by the removal of the claws.

If you let your declawed cat go outside, it will be at an increased risk of injury or death as it will not be able to defend itself in the way that nature intended. It cannot climb a tree to get away from a dog or other threat, and it cannot use its claw to defend itself against an attack.

As the outcry against declawing continues to mount, some veterinary surgeons are employing a supposedly more humane form of the surgery called tendonotomy, in which the tendon that allows the cat to extend its claws is severed. Although the claws are still in place, the cat can no longer use them. Although tendonotomy is less extreme than amputation of the claws, this crippling operation does not fit my definition of the word *humane*. Because the cat can no longer voluntarily remove the outer husks of the claws by itself with a natural scratching action as nature intended, owners must be attentive about keeping the claws trimmed.

Unfortunately, those owners who resort to surgery as a substitute for good training are rarely the type who can spare five minutes for maintenance of their cat's claws. Many veterinarians report that clients who opted for tendonotomy originally frequently come back in a few months to request the more drastic declawing surgery because they are tired of keeping up with the claw maintenance routine that tendonotomy requires. So these people are putting their cats through two painful procedures and two anesthesias, all because they will not spend the little bit of time it takes to train a cat to scratch properly in the first place!

SCRATCHING IS NATURAL

Scratching is as natural and necessary for cats as breathing. If you do not provide a place for your cat to scratch, you can be sure he will find a spot on his own. Some of my veterinarian friends have reported to me that many pet owners threaten to euthanize their cats if the vet will not perform declawing surgery. Is your sofa really more important to you than your cat's welfare? If your answer is yes, then you should not have a cat.

Scratching is vital to a cat's continued good health. When a cat plants his claws deep into a tree trunk and tugs, the act accomplishes several tasks. First, it removes the dull outer husk of the claw, revealing new, sharp claws. This is comparable to the human act of trimming our fingernails. Second, because each claw is attached to a tendon that allows it to extend and re-tract, the act of scratching actually exercises and tones those tendons and the associated muscles in the cat's neck, shoulders and back.

Cats also use scratching to mark their territory. You may not be aware of this fact but cats have special scent glands in the tips of their paws (as well as on their faces). When a cat "scratches" a particular spot, he is marking it with his scent to tell other cats that it is his own, just as when a cat rubs her face against its human companion it is telling you, quite affectionately, that you belong to him.

If you plan to get a cat, you must also make plans to provide an adequate scratching post and invest the bit of time required to train your cat that this is the proper place to scratch. I have one doorjamb in my home which all my cats use. They know it is their designated scratching spot and they do not scratch any-where else. If you are not willing to designate a doorjamb, just be sure you do provide some other suitable scratching surface.

Wood is a cat's preferred scratching surface because it firmly grips the claws' outer husks and facilitates their removal. If you make the mistake of providing your cat with a carpet-covered scratching post, you will be teaching him that soft materials are preferable for scratching, and he will choose your upholstered sofa or chair to sharpen his claws. However, if you provide some-thing hard, like a sisal-covered post or trimmed wooden tree trunk, then the cat will learn to scratch there and will always choose a hard surface. Proper training at an early age will spare your furniture.

It is also important to make sure that the scratching post you provide is stable. If it tips over every time your cat tries to use it, this will frighten your cat away and cause him to seek another spot to scratch. Make sure the base is wide and the post is sturdy enough to stand up to repeated scratching. The post must also be tall enough for your cat. Something that is suitable for kittens to scratch on may not work for adult cats. Check your local pet stores to locate a suitable post, or better still, find a nice, sturdy bit of tree trunk and bring that into your home. Not only will your cats love scratching on a tree trunk, but it will look nice in your home as well.

While your kitten is learning where to scratch, it may be helpful to keep a mister of plain water handy. If you see him scratching on the furniture or some other taboo spot, spray a mist of water at him while firmly saying, "No!" Then pick him up and take him to his scratching spot. When you see him scratching appropriately, be sure to lavish praise and attention on him for his good efforts. While training, never hit your pet or raise your voice, because human anger terrifies animals and makes them quite sad, because they cannot understand it. Be gentle and patient, and in time, your cat will learn where to scratch.

DECLAWING SHOULD BE OUTLAWED

The United States is one of the few industrialized nations that permits surgical declawing of cats. The procedure is illegal in the following nations: England, Scotland, Wales, Italy, France, Germany, Austria, Switzerland, Norway, Sweden, The Netherlands, Northern Ireland, Ireland, Denmark, Finland, Slovenia, Portugal, Belgium, Spain, Brazil, Australia, New Zealand, Yugoslavia, Israel, and Japan. So why does the United States, otherwise one of the more advanced nations in the world, allow such a cruel and barbaric procedure to be routinely performed?

Several groups are pressing for legislation to outlaw this inhumane and barbaric practice in the United States. Please write to your local legislators and see if they would be willing to sponsor bills at the state level to ban the practice of declawing. Together, we can make a difference, and save millions of animals from needless suffering.

TAIL DOCKING AND EAR CROPPING

There are many dog breeds, such as boxers and schnauzers, where kennel-club standards for the breed may call for a docked tail and cropped ears. I am absolutely opposed to subjecting any animal to a surgical procedure simply on the basis of changing its appearance to meet some archaic show standard. Natural ears and tails are best; that's the way that nature designed them and that's the way that we should leave them.

While such procedures are not nearly as painful as declawing, they still do represent a significant assault on your pet's emotional and physical feelings. These procedures may lead to a fear of veterinary visits or even of riding in the car, because your pet associates those visits with the pain of the surgery. Other behavioral problems may also surface, such as nervous biting. Do you really think it is worth it to subject your animal companion to such pain, particularly when you take into consideration the sort of side effects you may be triggering?

Please join me in saying no to these types of unnecessary surgical procedures. You will be sparing your pet a lot of pain and suffering and helping to educate others about the importance of caring for our animal companions in a humane and loving fashion.

Veterinary Care

If you have an animal companion, you must take responsibility for its health and well-being, which means annual veterinary checkups and routine vaccinations for rabies and whatever other shots your veterinarian might recommend for your particular locale. Before you select a veterinary doctor, check with friends whose opinion you trust to find out which veterinarians they use, and if there are any they specifically do not recommend.

It is important to establish a good working relationship with your veterinarian, and to let him or her get to know both you and your pet during regular office visits. That way, if a crisis does arise, the vet will already have an idea of your background, and will be able to diagnose and treat your pet more accurately.

Your vet will not only keep track of your pet's health, he will also be your partner in preventive maintenance, prescribing various medications to prevent heartworm and flea infestations, vaccinations to prevent serious disease and a nutritious diet to promote ongoing health. Your vet will maintain an individual file on each of your pets, with notes regarding any particular health problems that animal may have experienced.

If you cannot seem to establish a good working relationship with a particular vet, don't hesitate to seek out another doctor. It is vitally important to your pet's health that you work with a veterinarian who cares about him and about you. There are thousands of wonderful veterinarians out there; keep looking until you find the right one for you.

SOMETIMES, despite the best care in the world, your pet becomes ill. With the help of my angel guides, I have been able to heal many animals. In the next chapter, I will tell you how this gift was given to me and share some remarkable stories of animals who have regained their health after their owners brought them to me for treatment.

CHAPTER NINE

Healing with the Angels

When Your Pet Is Ill

*W*hen a beloved pet becomes ill or is injured, it can turn your world upside-down. Nothing makes a pet owner more desperate than being told their animal companion is terminally ill or mortally injured, and the best thing they can do is to put it out of its misery with euthanasia. Veterinarians save the lives of thousands of sick and injured animals every year, but there is only so much they can do. So, many clients bring an animal to me for healing after it is injured or diagnosed with a serious illness, and their veterinarians have told them there is no hope for recovery.

I did not come to animal healing lightly. I had to endure much pain and suffering in my own life to prepare me properly for the role I have today, and I had to be trained by my angel guides to correctly use the power they give me to heal the animals that are brought to me.

Of course, I cannot heal all injuries or cure all illness. Sometimes an animal is ready to pass over, and we should not interfere with its decision to go. This can be very difficult for some people who are determined to hang on to their pet at all costs. But often, they do not stop to consider the cost to the animal in terms of pain and suffering.

I do always recommend people continue with regular veterinary care even though most animals tell me they do not like going to the vet. In that respect they are like many people who don't like going to the doctor or dentist, but sometimes it is necessary and for their own good.

Though I can never promise what the outcome will be, healing always relieves pain. Sometimes there will be a complete recovery; for other animals, it is already their time to leave this earth and journey on. In these cases, there is nothing I can do, since all my healing power comes from my guides and its effectiveness varies in each individual case. But even when an animal passes over, I find I am still able to help grieving owners accept their loss and help them remember the many hours of joy their pet brought them during its life on earth.

I never cease to be amazed at the way my angel guides work through me. I am constantly being trained by them so that I may serve as an effective channel for their healing energy, and I have discovered that each guide has a different method of working. My main guide, Dr. David Thompson, was a battlefield surgeon during World War I. He taught me to work with energy and perform psychic operations. My second and newer guide, Harry Edwards, was a famous English healer who died in the fifties. He healed both animals and people. Harry sends healing energy through me and uses my body to direct healing vibrations to the animals I am working on.

I want to point out that guides do not work through humans without first asking for and being granted permission to do so.

I have given my guides permission to work through me, but I never allow my body to be completely taken over because I do not feel comfortable with that.

My guides have told me they must train to work in this dimension, so they will know how to heal through me. Older guides are used to visiting this dimension to work. Newer guides have to adjust to the energy frequencies on earth before they can work efficiently through a human physical body. When they first visit, they cannot stay for long because they tire, and the person they are working through tires also. As they adjust to the energy here, they are able to stay for longer periods of time.

I compare the experience of guides visiting this earth plane to men landing on the moon. On the moon, our astronauts were in a different atmosphere where they floated around and could not breathe without mechanical assistance, because they were not used to living in that dimension. So it is for my guides when they come to this dimension. It is important to remember that they do not have a physical body like we do. Their energy pulsates at a higher frequency than ours, so adjustments are necessary in order for them to be effective in their work here.

I must guard my energy to make sure I don't overwork myself. This is very important when you are doing the work that I do. I am working with both my physical and energy body when I heal, and would quickly become exhausted if I did not rest.

I have a great rapport with my two main healing guides. They both have an incredible sense of humor, and we often laugh together. Yet they are so different. One is infinitely patient and kind; the other is powerful and often has to restrain his strength to keep from shaking while we are healing. I am constantly overwhelmed by their love for us and all the members of the animal kingdom.

As I mentioned earlier, I have endured much pain over the

years. During the course of my life I have had fourteen surgeries. After a period of illness, including two major operations, I was told by my surgeon I would have to live the remainder of my life as a semi-invalid. After hearing the news, I was determined that in no way was that going to happen to me. I refused to accept the prognosis from my surgeon, and made up my mind that I was never going to have another operation again as long as I lived. I did not at that time realize that positive thinking could make me well, and that negative thinking and unhappiness had broken down my immune system and made my body sick.

Through positive thinking and determination, and by not accepting the doctor's sentence of life as a semi-invalid, I began my journey as a healer. I was determined to heal myself. I turned in another direction, away from despair to hope, from resignation to determination. Over the next two years, I steadily climbed back to good health. I was able to mend my body by seeing myself as constantly well. I now look back and feel as if that was another life, but I know it was an essential part of my training, all meant to prepare me for my eventual work as a healer and animal communicator.

Because I have experienced pain and self-healing in my own body, I know what it is like for animals. I put myself into their bodies and feel what they feel, so that it is easier for me to determine what is bothering them. Wherever they hurt, I hurt. Wherever they experience discomfort, I feel the same sensations in the corresponding part of my body. With the help of my guides, I am able to determine exactly what is bothering the animal and whether it can be healed. I do not have to guess.

Now I will tell you about some incredible animals and their owners whom I have been privileged to help within the last three years.

Magic

Mary Lynn Mombray was one of my first clients. One day, she rang me and said her cat, Magic, was ill and would probably have to have surgery. She asked to bring him to me for healing, saying the vet had told her he had heart problems.

She brought the cat to my studio, and I asked Magic for permission to help him feel better by putting my hands on him.

I always get down to the animal's level to connect with their energy so they feel comfortable. Though it takes a few minutes, usually they settle down in a spot underneath the table, on their owner's knee or on the sofa. Then I can work with them. Cats especially hate being taken out of their own environment so it takes them a little while longer to settle down.

First, I speak to them in a very soft voice and tell them how beautiful they are. I then ask for permission to stroke them and make them feel better. Magic was very laid back and relaxed. As I touched Magic, I started to feel the healing energy come through into my hands. I asked St. Francis to help me. When the energy comes through my hands, I get a tingling feeling and my hands become very warm and turn a golden color. This change is visible to the naked eye, and I have often had clients comment on the color of my hands as I work to heal their pet.

When I understand what is wrong with the animal, I put my hands on the part of the animal that is affected. I then wait for the lights that I use for healing to come down to me. I was given a beautiful blue indigo light to use on Magic.

I put my hands on the cat and could feel the vibrations going through the cat from the healing and the energy flowing from my guides through my hands. As I transmitted the energy, I felt the cat relaxing. All the animals I heal know that I am trying to

help them. They sense this on the telepathic level. I then visualized the blue light going all through the cat's body, cleansing
all the impurities and blockages from the heart.

I worked on Magic with my guides for about twenty minutes,
using blue, then gold and finally white lights to heal him. It may
take longer than twenty minutes with some animals, but that is
about the average length of time the healing energy flows. I work
on an animal until the energy doesn't come anymore, at which
point I realize my guides are finished.

This is just the first step. I also like to have a photograph of
each animal I am working with, so at night, when the universe
is still, I can continue to heal them. Some of my most powerful
healing is done at night, when I am distant (in the geographic
sense only) from the animals my guides and I are actually working upon. Before I go to sleep, I look at each photograph and
mentally prepare myself for the night's work. When I picked up
Magic's picture, I knew we were going to do more healing on
the cat that night.

Clients sometimes feel a bit strange about the absent healing
I do during the night. It's quite simple really. Normally, I am
wakened by my guides and go to work again. I use my mind
energy and am able to do healing on the sick or injured animal,
even though my physical body is still asleep. I also converse
telepathically with the animals I am healing. I tell them what I
am going to do and they are completely willing and understand.
I then go back to them and give more of a boost to the healing.
The only difference is that I am not actually there; I do it through
visualization. And my guides are always working with me, particularly on the animals that are very sick.

Sometimes absent healing goes on for a week, and sometimes
it is necessary to get people to bring their animals back in again

for hands-on healing. My guides tell me what is necessary for each individual case. They diagnose and decide on a course of treatment, much like any veterinarian would.

Magic required only one more absent healing session. Within a week, he had completely recovered and Mary Lynn reported they had no further problems.

Funa

For five years, Mary Denney had visited one veterinarian after another, trying to find out what was wrong with her cat, Funa. No one could determine what ailed the cat, which suffered with constant digestive disturbances. He'd been sick for so long Mary couldn't remember when he'd been well. He often couldn't keep food in his stomach and vomited almost everything he was fed. He was thin and lethargic. During the long time he had been ill, no doctor had been able to diagnose the cat's illness. Mary was fearful the cat might die soon.

Mary called me in desperation after hearing me speak about animal communication at a gathering for people interested in metaphysics. She told me about her cat and asked if I could help. This was very soon after the beginning of my training as a healer and I was not sure what I could do, but I agreed to try.

I closed my eyes and asked Dr. Thompson if he could help me with the cat. I connected to both of Mary's cats through my energy and visualized where they slept at night. I described the scene for Mary who confirmed what I was seeing was accurate. One of the cats told me he loved to have his head rubbed while the other didn't. Mary confirmed this was true, also.

I started to concentrate on Funa and immediately began to feel physically ill in my body. The sick cat told me he had been ill for a long time and was dying. He was in a state of panic about his illness. I smelled a chemical smell and knew the cat's illness had been caused by swallowing something. The cat sent me a picture of Mary's laundry room and I knew something had happened to Funa there. I felt the cat's illness was due to some sort of chemical exposure and told Mary so. I wondered if it was possible the cat had swallowed some chemical, because I could feel the lining of its intestines to be very sore and raw, which had resulted in the chronic digestive disturbances the cat had suffered for so long.

"Has Funa by any chance licked up some bleach?" I asked Mary.

Mary became excited, telling me that five years before, the cat had fallen into a washing machine full of bleach, but she hadn't realized at the time that it had swallowed any of the deadly and caustic poison. I realized the bleach had caused extensive damage to the cat's stomach and intestinal lining and that damage was what had made him chronically ill for the past five years.

I then called on my guides to help me heal the cat. Dr. Thompson came forward to assist me and instructed and guided me in the healing operation. I visualized a laser beam cutting the cat open and lights were given to me to work with. As each light was handed to me, I was told what to do. After the cat was opened up, I could actually see how ulcerated its stomach was, and I knew how desperately sick the animal truly was. I saw a beautiful golden light and knew it was meant to help me heal the cat. I visualized the light healing and repairing the cat's stomach lining. I pushed energy through the cat's intestines with the golden light, pushing out all the sickness.

After the gold, I was given a beautiful blue light, and told to visualize this going all through the intestines, soothing and healing the damage. I used the laser beam to suture the cat closed, and bathed his entire body with another beautiful light, violet blue this time, and left the cat in that light to protect him as he continued to heal. Mary reported that the cat had fallen into a deep sleep during the course of the operation. I myself felt exhausted as the work of healing the cat drained all my energy.

That night, my guides wakened me at three A.M. and I knew my work with Funa was not finished. I felt my energy body joining with the universal energy stream on the astral plane. I visualized my astral hands and my mind energy healing the body of the sick cat while it slept. I was very aware of my guides working with me.

Mary reported the cat was visibly recovered the next day, with a much improved appetite. For the next two weeks, my guides and I continued to do healing on Funa every night. Mary reported that the cat had made a complete recovery. It was gaining weight and had a normal appetite once again.

Mr. Clinker

I had become a regular guest on the Scott Cluthe radio show in Houston. Each time I was on, the phone bank lit up with calls from pet owners eager to recover a lost pet, or to solve some behavioral or health problem. I soon found I was quickly able to connect with the animals in question through the owner's energy. I often talked to the animals live on the air, telling the owners things only they would know about their animals, such as having an operation or illness, or the fact that this was not the animal's first home or that their previous owner was cruel to them. The astounded owners always confirmed as accurate whatever I relayed to them from their pets, though they couldn't begin to understand how I knew what I knew.

A man named Irwin called one day very distressed about his cat, Mr. Clinker, who had been diagnosed with terminal feline leukemia. Mr. Clinker had a large tumor on his jaw. The vet said the tumor could be removed, but because of its size and location, the lower jaw would be lost. Irwin declined the disfiguring surgery, unwilling to put his beloved pet through so much suffering. In his own words, he instituted a "death watch."

Daily, the tumor grew in size, causing Mr. Clinker terrible pain. He snored and experienced bouts of apnea that meant he had trouble breathing. His appetite faded to nothing. One day, quite by chance, Irwin tuned in to the Scott Cluthe show and caught the very end of the program. He called immediately, and I spoke to him after the broadcast ended. Despite Houston's vastness, Irwin happened to live within walking distance of my home, which was fortunate as he could not drive due to poor vision. I went to see Mr. Clinker at Irwin's home.

When I arrived, I was astounded to see a garden full of art, including a lovely bronze figure. Irwin turned out to be the proverbial starving artist, a man who had very little money, but a heart full of love and compassion for animals. He had taken in eight cats whom he fed and doted upon.

I was alarmed when I saw the size of the large tumor on Mr. Clinker's jaw. When I connected with the cat, I realized he was still a bit wild. Because he was so very sick, Irwin had put him into his own room where the other cats could not disturb him. I felt Mr. Clinker's energy and waited for the cat to accept my presence. It took him a little while, and I realized the cat was prone to hiss and spit. I asked the cat if I could help him and told him I would be very honored if he allowed me to do so. Mr. Clinker thought about it for a while, then replied that he would allow me to help. Again, I felt the wonderful warm energy coming into my hands and knew healing power was already being transmitted.

I put my hands on Mr. Clinker and he offered no resistance.

I felt in my own throat how very sore the cat's throat was. I felt the blood disorder, which Irwin had identified as leukemia. I could see a beautiful green light coming down and knew this was the one I would use to heal the cat. I took the green light from the eyes down through the neck and the rest of Mr. Clinker's body, and while drawing it through I could feel the vibrations within the cat's body and knew healing was taking place. I imagined the impurities all being taken from his blood and his blood being healthy and well and fit. I talked to him and told him he too must imagine this, seeing himself whole and healthy and well.

I then started healing the cat's throat and his jaw. I was again given a beautiful healing light, this time royal blue, which I visualized on his throat. At the same time, healing energy was being passed through my hands.

Mr. Clinker was feeling very relaxed. The healing continued for some twenty minutes, then I felt the energy withdraw from my hands and knew the healing had been completed for that session. I thanked Mr. Clinker and told Irwin I would be doing more healing at night. Mr. Clinker also required several more hands-on healing sessions. I asked Irwin to keep me informed of the cat's progress.

Irwin was delighted with the results as Mr. Clinker seemed to be recovering well after three days. Then he took Mr. Clinker to his regular vet the next week, and other than a little ulceration secondary to a minor throat inflammation, there was absolutely no indication of the large tumor that just the week before had threatened to end the cat's life. Mr. Clinker was fully and completely cured.

Mr. Clinker lived another eleven months after my guides healed him, free of pain and without obvious signs of illness. When Irwin took the cat to the vet, the tumor was no longer

visible on Mr. Clinker's jaw. He had a healthy appetite and re-
newed vigor for life. Then one night he passed to the other side
in his sleep, having reached the ripe old cat age of seventeen
years.

Jean Lafitte

My friend Pat's son Carter had been greatly disappointed to discover he couldn't fit his new "pirate turtle" out with a brass
earring and peg-leg, but nonetheless, Jean Lafitte had turned out
to be a most satisfactory pet. Pat's family had owned the turtle
for almost two years, and in that time, his shell had grown from
less than two inches to more than six inches across.

During the first cold snap of 1993, Jean Lafitte quit eating.
This was puzzling because he'd always had quite an appetite. Pat
phoned the vet and he told her that when turtles get cold, they
often go off their food. He advised her to move the aquarium
away from the window where it might be drafty to a more se-
cluded spot inside the house. She moved it to her dining room,
which has no exterior windows.

But the move didn't help. Jean Lafitte still wouldn't eat.
Within a few days, he started to drift aimlessly in his tank,
spewing mucus from both nostrils. Pat's son was terribly upset
and she felt panicked, wondering what to do to restore the turtle
to good health. It had now been seven days since it had eaten
anything.

That morning, I'd made arrangements to meet Pat, but she
was distracted and worried about the turtle, and she couldn't
concentrate.

I immediately picked up on Pat's distress and asked her what
was wrong. She told me, and I offered to speak to the turtle and
find out what was wrong, an offer which astounded her. Pat had

no idea what I was talking about. Though we had been friends for more than a year, I had never mentioned my ability to communicate with animals to her.

Briefly, I described my telepathic gift. Though Pat was quite skeptical, she felt so desperate she would have tried anything to save the turtle.

I asked Pat for the turtle's name. When she told me, "Jean Lafitte," I couldn't help but reply, "That's quite a posh name for a turtle."

"He's quite a posh turtle," Pat responded, still not sure of the value of this experiment.

I closed my eyes and within moments, I was able to tell Pat that the turtle was quite unhappy about its tank being moved from its accustomed spot in her son's bedroom window. He wanted it moved back immediately. Pat was amazed because she had only just moved the tank a few days before and hadn't mentioned it to me.

The turtle told me he was dying. He told me he was very sad because he loved Pat's family and did not want to leave them. Then he started to give me a laundry list of the things that were wrong in his habitat, all things that had contributed, along with the cold weather, to his illness.

Speaking in a small, tinny voice, he told me he had outgrown his aquarium tank, and that it didn't have any stones on the bottom where he could get proper traction to walk and dive. He sent me a picture of his feet slipping on the bottom of the tank. He also informed me his water needed to be much deeper so he could swim, and filtrated to stay fresher and cleaner. "As long as I was a small turtle, this tank was fine, but now I am too big for it and have no room to swim and the water gets dirty too quickly," the turtle told me. Finally, Jean Lafitte asked for a larger rock for basking and diving, a green plant and a small fish for a companion.

Pat quickly drove to the nearest pet store to rescue the turtle, though she was still feeling quite unconvinced of the wisdom of what she was doing. I have quite a sense of humor, and I think Pat wondered if she hadn't become the unwitting victim of an elaborate prank. To encourage her as she left, I emphasized again that speed was necessary as the turtle was near death.

While Pat was in the store, she made the mistake of telling the pet store owner she was buying the goldfish for her turtle. He looked at her like she was crazy and told her, "Lady, you can't put a goldfish into a tank with a turtle. He'll eat it."

"Oh, no," Pat assured him. "My turtle told me he just wants the fish for a friend."

"Your turtle told you what?" the man said, looking at Pat even more strangely.

Pat turned her head as if she hadn't heard him and hurried out of the store with her $79.53 worth of turtle goods, thinking it was all an act of futility, that it was too late and the turtle was going to die anyway, and she'd be stuck with an elaborate turtle habitat and no bread or milk for her children for the rest of the week.

Pat set up the new aquarium in her son's bedroom window and moved the turtle into his new home. For the next three days, she hovered over Jean Lafitte, watching closely for some sign of improvement. There was none, but at least he didn't get any sicker; he was still alive.

On the fourth day, the turtle ate two sticks of turtle food and Pat noticed his nose was no longer running. She and her children celebrated this obvious turn for the better and called to inform me of the good news.

Jean Lafitte continued to improve. By the seventh day, he was swan-diving off his new basking rock and marching around his tank like some lord of the deep, fully recovered. Pat called and thanked me profusely, still not quite sure what she was thanking me for, but knowing that somehow, I was at least partly responsible for saving the turtle's life. She didn't understand it, but to her credit, she accepted it. That was Pat's introduction to the world of animal communication.

Unfortunately, the goldfish had become a bit more relaxed too, losing that look of sheer terror he'd assumed when he first realized he was confined in a ten-gallon tank with a turtle. One evening when Pat came home, she went to greet Jean Lafitte and noticed there was no goldfish in the tank. She looked everywhere, but there simply weren't that many places for a goldfish to hide in the tank. In a panic, she called me and I immediately connected to Jean Lafitte, asking him where the goldfish was.

"I've eaten him," he replied. "I knew I would never get the fish if I'd told you I was going to eat him."

I chastised him for misrepresenting the real reason he wanted the fish. To this day, I haven't forgiven myself for my role in the hapless goldfish's death. He really deceived me, that turtle. I didn't realize he was so crafty. He told me he wanted a friend, when all he wanted was a filet!

For her part, Pat thinks that perhaps there were some nutrients, minerals or vitamins in that fish that Jean Lafitte needed to complete his recovery. At any rate, she hasn't given him any more fish to munch upon, and he continues to be a very, happy healthy turtle. As often happens with animals I help, John Lafitte has turned into a regular gossip and now keeps me informed of all the goings-on in Pat's house, especially noticing when she fails to wash up the dishes. Pat just wishes he would quit telling me when she hasn't done the laundry.

Beau

My friend Donna brought her dog, Beau, to me for healing. She had taken him to the veterinarian because he was limping, but the doctor said Beau's problems were the result of his advanced age and he could do nothing to help him. When I connected to Beau's energy, I picked up all five of Donna's pets. A cat named Spankie came forward and informed me that Beau suffered terribly with the pain in his feet and legs, but tried to hide his pain because he didn't want to worry his family.

I inquired after the dog's health, and Donna said she believed everything was alright, but she worried because Beau had real difficulty getting going in the morning sometimes.

Spankie was clamoring to be heard again. "Beau's feet do hurt him. He does not want Mommy to know, but I am the biggest kitty and when I speak, no one talks back to me. Beau has taken care of all of us for a long time, so now I am going to take care of Beau by telling his secret."

I told Donna what the cat had said, that the dog suffered with his feet but kept his pain hidden because he didn't want to worry her. With Donna's permission, I started healing the dog, who quickly regained his former boisterous and active nature. The quietness and inactivity Donna had put down to the onset of maturity was actually due to the pain from Beau's congenital foot problem. Once my guides relieved the dog's pain, he became his old self again.

There is an interesting "foot" note to this story. Donna brought Beau in several more times for healing, along with his brother Cody who had an ear problem. I noticed both dogs had skin rashes, which Donna said their vet had not been able to clear up. I asked my guides for help and they told me that both dogs were allergic to the wheat in their food. I advised Donna to switch to a diet of rice and fish for her dogs and the skin rash disappeared from both dogs within a matter of weeks.

Beau has since died of old age, but it gave Donna great comfort to see the relief from pain my guides were able to give him, making his last few months comfortable and productive.

Heidi

Over the Christmas holidays of 1995, my dear friend Valerie Patrick called me in a panic about her beautiful German shepherd, Heidi. She'd been having some health problems and the veterinarian who examined her found she had a tumor on the right side of her back. The doctor wanted to do a biopsy, but Val didn't consent to the procedure because the previous summer Heidi had suffered two mild heart attacks following anesthesia for a constriction in her throat. The anesthesia was too strong and it weakened Heidi's heart.

Heidi managed for a while, but it was obvious she didn't have her usual strength and vigor. Finally, Val called me in distress at two A.M. one morning. Heidi had suffered a third heart attack, much more serious this time. I went and laid my hands on Heidi, and sent healing energy coursing through her body. She recovered, but she was still very weak, so I continued to work on her.

Val had some friends come through from Canada. They immediately noticed the growth on Heidi's back, which by then was about the size of a walnut and quite prominent, with hairs sticking out all around it. Val said everyone who came to visit noticed it. Val knew she was going to have to do something about the tumor, but she hated to take Heidi in for another operation because of what had happened the last time.

I started directing healing energy through the tumor, visualizing it shrinking in size and being absorbed harmlessly into

Heidi's body. I worked on her with absent healing every night for several weeks. Six weeks later, Val looked for the tumor, but it was gone. Val called Ruby, her maid, and asked her which side Heidi's tumor was on. Ruby looked at Heidi and said, "It's gone!" There was no trace of the tumor to be found.

A week later, Heidi was scheduled for her regular dental checkup. The vet looked for the tumor to check it and found it wasn't there. He asked Val which vet had performed the surgery to remove the growth, all while madly looking for the scar and stitches. Val didn't know if he was a believer but decided to tell him she had the surgery done psychically. Predictably, the vet thought she was crazy.

"Are you sure you didn't go to another doctor to have it removed?" the vet asked her.

Val is very spiritual and we've been friends for twenty-one years, but she says she sometimes still can't believe it herself that healing energy from my guides restored Heidi to good health without veterinary intervention.

Normally, as I have stated earlier, I recommend working with veterinarians and continuing regular veterinary care as well as using healing energy. But in this case, Heidi had shown a marked sensitivity to anesthesia, and I knew a surgical procedure would do her more harm than good, and perhaps even kill her. I am thankful I was able to use the healing energy of my guides to heal my friend's dog.

Bravo

A family called me in great distress. Their beloved cat Bravo was ill, but they did not specify the illness for me. They were very skeptical of my ability to help their cat, but consulted me, as many clients do, out of desperation.

When they arrived, I placed my hands on the cat and knew he was full of worms, but oddly, not worms common to cats. Bravo's owners confirmed he had worms. They had just come from the vet, who was not able to do anything for the cat because the case was too far advanced.

I asked Bravo if he had eaten anything unusual, and he sent me a picture of a dead possum, so I knew the source of the worm infestation. I also knew the cat was very ill. The worms had formed a sort of ball, which was causing a life-threatening intestinal blockage.

Working with my guides, we removed the worms and cured Bravo completely. His owners were thrilled to have their cat restored to good health.

People often ask me when I say I remove something, if I actually see what is being removed. Usually I don't, because the tumor or damaged area is being cleansed with healing lights provided to me by my guides. The healing energy is directed through my hands, which feel tingly and warm while this is happening. At times, the energy flow put through to heal an animal will be so strong it causes my hands to vibrate.

So when I say I remove worms, I don't actually see them. I know only that my guides have removed worms that have been diagnosed by a veterinarian, and when the cat is taken back for a checkup, the worms are no longer there. The one exception I can remember is the intestinal blockage I discovered in Zuki, the iguana (from chapter 6).

Crystal

One of my favorite stories of healing concerns a cat brought to me by my client Beverly, who rescues cats. At any given time,

Beverly has fifty or more cats in her care and I often help her by collecting food, towels, and blankets from my clients.

This cat, which Beverly called Crystal, had no fur whatsoever, and its entire body was covered with open, weeping sores. The vet diagnosed her with a virus, which he says she caught from her mother. He recommended putting the animal to sleep to put it out of its misery.

When I connected to the cat, I realized she was in extreme pain. I asked, as I always do, for her permission to begin healing, and the cat agreed, requesting only that I not touch her because she was in so much pain. I reassured Crystal I would not put my hands on her. Her wounds looked so dreadful I would have been afraid to do so for fear of causing her even more pain.

I started to heal the cat through its aura, sending healing light through by holding my hands about two inches away from her body. I healed Crystal with absent healing every night for a week, and then Beverly returned with the cat to my studio. At first, I thought the cat hadn't made much progress, then I felt a surge of strength go through my body and realized she had grown stronger. I was encouraged. It was given to me to tell Beverly to start putting antiseptic ointment on the sores and feed the cat a diet of plain boiled rice and fish.

When Beverly returned the following week, it was obvious Crystal was feeling much better. The sores were healing and there were tufts of fur starting to grow in patches. I saw Crystal once more, then continued absent healing for several weeks. Now Crystal is completely healthy. Her sores are all healed and she has a full coat of beautiful beige fur and is ready to be placed in an adoptive home.

* * *

A lost pet is just as upsetting for pet owners as having a sick pet. In some ways, it is even more distressing, because you are never quite sure what has happened to your pet if you can't find it. In the next chapter, I will share some stories of lost pets, and give pointers for the best course to follow if your pet should stray.

CHAPTER TEN

Where, Oh Where Has My Little Dog Gone?

Lost Pets

When a pet is lost, it can be devastating to a family. The frantic neighborhood search, the posters tacked to light poles, the walking and calling your pet's name in vain, can fray even the steadiest nerves.

The first thing I do when a pet is missing is calm the owners and get them to give me as much information as possible about the lost pet. While they are talking, they usually focus and settle down sufficiently for me to connect to their lost pet through their energy.

Happily, in the majority of cases I pick up the animal right away. The ones who are truly lost are always confused and frightened, and eager to find their way back home. On the other hand, the ones who have left home by choice will not even consider going back, particularly cats, which are far less tolerant of ill treatment from their humans than dogs are. At the very least, I can gather enough information from the lost animal for its owners to launch a targeted search. In some cases, we will be lucky and find the animal, but sadly, I cannot find all lost animals. I can only do so much. The owner is the one who has to go out and put up posters in the target area and find the landmarks I give them from pictures the animals send me.

The joy I feel when I succeed in recovering an animal is incredible because I know the odds are against the animal ever being found. Prayer, good luck, and the ability of the missing animal to communicate with pictures and feelings are my strongest allies in the search. Some animals communicate more clearly than others, and that is always a big help.

We've all read stories of incredible journeys undertaken by lost pets trying to find their families. Some such journeys can cover hundreds of miles. We even hear of animals tracking their families across country.

A very famous case more than twenty years ago involved a family that moved from New York to California, leaving their year-old black-and-white cat in the care of a neighboring family until they could get settled in their new home and send for him. The cat had a very unusual marking on his stomach, which appeared to be a perfect outline of the continental United States. Unfortunately, he ran away within a few days after the move, and the neighbors called their friends in California to tell them of the disappearance.

Thirteen months later, across more than three thousand miles of rugged terrain, through all kinds of weather and dangers, a scraggly black-and-white cat with what appeared to be a map of the United States on its stomach showed up at the family's back door in California, meowing to be let in. This heroic feat catapulted the feline to brief fame, with his picture appearing in newspapers all over the country.

But how did this remarkable cat find his family? How did he know where to go when he had never even seen their new home or have any idea exactly where they were moving? The answer is that he tracked their energy. The bond between the cat and his family was so strong he was literally able to use their energy as a lifeline during the long months he was separated from them.

People always want to know: How do lost animals find their way home? Why is it that some succeed in their quest and others do not?

There's quite a bit of science involved in the answers to these questions, which I will try to explain clearly so that you may understand how the homing instinct works in animals.

You already know we are all surrounded by energy. Energy in its purest form is the life force of the universe. It flows around us and through us. In fact, our bodies are energy arranged in solid form. In the popular science-fiction film *Star Wars,* this energy was called "the force," and I must say George Lucas's concept of how energy fields work is not far off the mark.

You also know that animals communicate telepathically, using their mind energy to transmit pictures, thoughts and feelings back and forth. We do this also, though unknowingly, and it is this constant stream of mind energy we put out back and forth through the electromagnetic fields of the earth that our pets use to track their way back to us. Even though your animal is lost, he can still pick up the thoughts and feelings transmitting out through your energy. The energy link is not broken even though the physical link may well be.

Like humans, animals have varying degrees of intelligence and sensitivity. Some humans can cook or draw or play the piano, while many others can't do any of these things. So it is with animals. Some can tune in quite easily to their owners' thoughts and feelings; others are not as adept.

Sometimes an animal's willingness to communicate depends upon the motivation of the moment. If your pet has left home because he is angry or jealous of a new arrival, he may not be nearly as eager to reunite with you as you are with him. Other animals are overcome by fear and decide it is safer to stay in their new location than risk the dangers of an attempted journey home, while others are confident enough to trust all their senses and tune in to the energy fields where they will be able to pick up the mind energy you are constantly transmitting.

Remember, you already have an energy link with your pet because you have lived together and established a pattern of communication. That energy link is just like a radio wave. You can tune your energy in to that of your pet like you were tuning in a radio station. Each time you think of your pet, he is on the receiving end of the thought, almost as if you were calling him on the telephone. The only difference is that you are probably not attuned to the energy line like your pet is, so you don't "hear" him when he communicates with you.

If an animal is trying to reunite with its family, it will instinctively tune in to vibrations in the universal energy fields. Some animals have a heightened awareness of their senses that functions like a built-in compass, and they can feel the pull of a particular direction when they tune in to your energy. Other animals do not have this ability, and when I tune in to them, I can feel their confusion and fear. A fearful, confused animal is much more difficult to recover than a brave and confident one, because the fearful animal will not take the steps it must take to find its way home. The truth is, only a small percentage of lost animals ever find their way home.

Many times, particularly in the case of valuable animals, a pet hasn't been lost; it's been stolen, and you can be sure those responsible for the theft will do everything in their power to make sure they aren't discovered. I have the best chance of finding an animal that has truly been lost, who can provide me good information in the form of images and feelings about their journey from home, which I can then reconstruct to send the owners on a targeted search for their pet. Some will remember more clearly the route they have taken while others will be confused. If they are confused, that confusion is all they can send me, so it becomes very difficult for me to get any information about their location.

If I am lucky, the animal will be able to send me a picture of a very distinctive landmark. I had a client whose cat, Jaspar, was able to send me an image of a church with a dark green roof that he said was nearby. Though the church was more than ten miles away, the owner was able to retrieve his cat because the location and identity of that particular building were unmistakable.

Sometimes, when a cat has been chasing a bird or a dog has been chasing a squirrel, they are so preoccupied that they lose track of their surroundings. When they realize they are in unfamiliar territory, they become disoriented and panicky. These cases are difficult to resolve also, because during the chase, the animal was paying no attention to his route, only to his prey, so they cannot give me many landmarks or clues to their location.

Workmen visiting your home present another danger. They often leave their trucks open while they are working, and cats cannot seem to resist investigating an open door. I had a client whose cat hitched a ride in a carpet-cleaning truck. When the workers opened the back of their truck at their office in the next town, fourteen miles from the woman's home, a cat jumped out. The workmen thought nothing of it until the woman called the next day to ask if they had seen her cat. Though she put up posters near their office, she got no response and presumed her cat was lost forever. Then, eight weeks later he showed up at her door, a bit thin but in perfect health.

The same is true when a pet has been frightened by another

animal. A cat who has been chased for several blocks by a large dog is not only confused but terrified, and in mortal fear for its life. In these cases, when I connect to their energy I tell them to stay right where they are, calm themselves and gather their energy. Then I tell them to wait until the universe is still and dark (night), when I will waken and tune in to their energy. I reassure them and tell them to trust their instincts. I reinforce the idea that they are a very smart dog or cat, who can easily find their way home under the cover of darkness.

I tune in to them with my ears, so they receive the idea that they must use their ears to check for any noise before they cross a street. If there is noise (a car approaching) I tell them they must be very still and wait for it to be quiet again before crossing. I send the message telepathically with my mind, but also with my body, so the animal knows what he must do to travel safely.

Sometimes they find the courage to start their journey home. It may take a few days or even a few weeks, but usually I can get some of these animals home. A lot depends on the animal's personality, whether he is brave and not overanxious. If the journey home seems too daunting, they will often stay in their new location and find themselves loving homes.

Many animals become lost because their owner assumes they will be safe no matter what. You should never let your dog or cat roam freely; not only might they get lost, they could also be hit by a car, stolen, or attacked by another animal. It is your responsibility as a pet owner to see to the safety and security of your animal. If your dog has proven himself capable of jumping over a high fence or digging under to escape your yard, you must make whatever changes are necessary to provide him a secure place. Try to send him pictures of the dangers that await in the world outside his fence. If dogs and cats only knew how dangerous the world can be, most of them would never leave their doors. But like children, animals are filled with a sense of adventure that all too often is not accompanied by sufficient caution.

Dogs need walking every day. They need to get out and exercise regularly. Don't feel that just because you have a big yard that is sufficient. Animals are curious about their world, and need to see and understand the world around them. Walking also orients them to their neighborhood so that it becomes familiar and not as frightening to them.

Be especially vigilant about your pet's safety when you go on vacation. If you choose to leave your animal behind, I recommend you hire a knowledgeable pet sitter rather than rely on your neighbors to care for your pet. A few years ago, hardly anyone had heard of a pet sitter, but now they are becoming more popular as people are beginning to realize that being left in a kennel can be a very unhappy experience for an animal. Not only must they endure the stress of all the other cooped-up, frightened, and lonely animals barking and yowling, they may also be exposed to contagious diseases or pick up fleas in such an atmosphere.

Animals that have been put in a kennel have no idea why they are there. They don't know if it is a punishment, or if they are to be left there indefinitely. It's like us going to prison. Suddenly, they go from a comfortable bed and large yard, to sleeping on damp concrete and confined to a cage that barely has enough room for them to turn around in. I have treated many behavior problems in animals that cropped up after the pet was left in a kennel for a week or so.

So, take the time to locate and interview a reliable pet sitter. Ask for references, just as you would if you were leaving your children with someone new. Tell the sitter about your pet's routine, and stress the importance of maintaining that routine. Be sure and explain to your animal that you will be leaving for just a little while, but that someone very nice will come and look after them while you are gone. It is a great comfort to animals when their owners take the time to tell them what is going to happen. That way, they do not get so nervous and confused.

MOVING is a very dangerous time for cat owners, as cats have a tendency to form an energy link with their physical location (e.g. your old house). Domestic felines can use that energy link with something scientists call "psi tracking," to find their way back to their original home, even if it is thousands of miles away. Though scientists have a name for this ability, they don't understand how it works or why cats are equipped with this particular skill.

Remember to confine your cat to one room of your new home for at least a week after you move. The week of confinement allows cats time to form an energy link with their new location, so that when you let them out into the rest of the house, they will be content to stay and not try to roam or run back to their old house.

1 have many clients who ask me why all the stray cats in the world arrive on their doorstep. It isn't by accident. It's because they are cat lovers and cats looking for a new home will track positive energy vibrations to a house where they know a cat lover is in residence. Like a radio wave is picked up by a receiver tuned to the proper channel, cats tune in to the energy vibrations of a cat lover to locate your house, knowing full well they will be welcomed, however reluctantly. They also know, from reading

your energy vibrations, that if they stick around long enough they will be regularly fed and well-cared for.

Technology has brought us a new way to track and recover lost or stolen pets. It is a tiny microchip, first developed to provide irrefutable proof of identity for expensive horses and exotic birds, but it wasn't long before the veterinary community caught on to the usefulness of the idea for their own clientele. The microchip is programmed with a unique identifying code and then injected into your pet with a special hypodermic needle. The newer and more expensive devices can actually be used to track an animal on a geographic map, just like something you would see in a spy movie. The older ones simply provide proof of identity for a recovered animal.

The problem is that there is currently no standard for identification. Your local animal shelter may subscribe to one of these programs, but not another. Still, if you allow your pet to roam freely, it might be a good idea to invest in one of these tracking devices. But remember, no device can do the job you as a pet owner must do, which is to provide your animal with a loving, safe, and secure environment, so be vigilant in the care of your pet.

Humane workers believe strongly in county registration programs in which an ordinance requires you to register your pet for a nominal onetime fee. You are then given a tag to put on your pet's collar. If your pet happens to get lost, the information on the tag will give humane workers all they need to reunite your pet with your family. In counties where these registration programs are in force, there is a much higher rate of animals being returned to their owners.

*   *   *

Now I will share some stories of lost pets and their owners, and how we recovered them and reunited them with their families.

Sugar

Carol Moore has a beloved Maltese named Sugar. One day, someone accidentally left the garden gate ajar and Sugar got out. Carol was frantic with worry because she lives close to a major thoroughfare and was afraid Sugar might get hit by a car.

Carol had heard about me through a friend, so she phoned immediately to tell me of Sugar's disappearance. While I was looking at a picture of Sugar, the dog began to communicate with me, relating details of Carol's life that only Sugar, but certainly not I, could know. Carol was overwhelmed with an incredible feeling of relief, knowing that her dog was well and communicating with me.

Sugar told me her journey began after she left Carol's yard. I was able to pick up Carol's house and garden in great detail. I saw the gate ajar and also told Carol I saw a freeway opposite the house to the right. Then Sugar started to tell me about her journey.

First, she went across the road, being careful to avoid the cars. She told me a woman in a cream-colored car then picked her up and put her into her car. Next, she complained because her "mommy," as she referred to Carol, always had a nice, soft towel folded on the car seat for her to rest upon, and there was no towel in this woman's car. She transmitted to my body a feeling of unsteadiness, particularly in my arms and legs, and I knew she'd had difficulty staying on the car seat because the woman's upholstery was slippery. When I told Carol about the towel, she became very excited because she did keep a towel on the car seat for Sugar.

Sugar said they had passed a church on the way, and transmitted a picture of the church to me. She also sent a picture of a supermarket on the left side of the road. Then she transmitted a feeling with her body of the car turning to the left shortly after the supermarket.

Somewhere after the left turn, Sugar sensed the car turning right, and then it pulled into a garage and stopped. She sent this information to me telepathically.

I did not feel any hunger or thirst in Sugar's body, so I knew the people who had picked her up were feeding and watering her. Sugar then told me she was inside a house and flashed me a picture of the home's interior, a cream room with a fireplace. It comforted Carol a lot to know her beloved dog was being looked after, and that she was safe.

A man in the house kept saying to the lady who had picked up Sugar, "Let's take the dog back. We have her name on her collar and her owner's address. Let's take her back." But his wife and children wanted to keep her because she was so pretty. Sugar kept sending me images of the home's interior. Sugar was afraid she might not see Carol again, because the man kept repeating, "Give the dog back," and the woman kept answering, "No."

I told Carol the only way to get Sugar back was to start praying that the family who had the dog would open their hearts and give her back. I told Carol to put up posters with Sugar's picture and an offer of a reward in the area near the family's house, so Carol re-created Sugar's journey in her car and found the church and the supermarket, just as her pet had described.

Carol had posters made and put them up as I suggested. Late in the afternoon of that same day, Carol received a phone call from a little girl who said they had bought a dog from someone, and this dog had an ID tag. The girl asked if Carol owned a white dog named Sugar, but before Carol could answer, the phone went dead.

Carol was hysterical and thought, "How could they do that to me?" But as I had suggested, she calmed herself, focused and prayed for her dog's speedy return. I had also told her to have all her friends pray for Sugar's return. Prayer is very powerful, particularly when your pet is lost. The more friends you have praying for your pet's return, the better.

Twenty minutes after the phone call, Carol's doorbell rang and there stood a little girl with Sugar. Carol was overjoyed as she took her dog into her arms. She looked outside to see the girl's father who was in a cream-colored car as Sugar had mentioned. Carol was amazed when she saw the car just as I described it, and vowed to be more careful about making sure that the gate was securely fastened before she let Sugar into the garden unattended.

Madonna

One day I had an unusual phone call from a woman by the name of Salise Shuttlesworth, requesting my help in finding a family of pigs. A former attorney who had given up her practice to devote herself to the care of orphaned and abandoned animals, Salise is executive director of a no-kill animal shelter in Houston called "Special Pals." The family of pigs had been stolen from this shelter. Although the theft had been on television and in the newspapers, and Salise had issued numerous appeals for the return of her beloved animals, no one responded. My daughter, Emma, set up an appointment with Salise, who came in right away armed with pictures of her pigs.

When I attempted to establish a telepathic connection with the animals, I was particularly drawn to the energy of the mother pig, Madonna. I couldn't establish a clear link with the piglets, but this did not surprise me. Just as it takes a while for human infants to learn how to talk, infant animals must learn how to communicate telepathically.

As I tuned in to Madonna's energy, I felt a great sadness. I asked her why she was unhappy and she told me one of her babies had died at birth because she had accidentally stepped on it. It made her very sad. She was frightened for her babies and was concerned for their welfare, and for herself and the piglets' father, Dick.

I told Salise to first inform the slaughterhouses about the pigs but she had already done this. She was amazed when I told her about the baby pig that had died at birth. She knew I was truly in touch with her pets.

I asked Madonna what she could tell me about the night she and her family had been taken. She sent me a picture of two men who had come in a truck. She transmitted the color black, so I knew it was the middle of the night and not the early morning when the pigs were stolen. I got the feeling Madonna knew one of the men who had taken them. Then she told me one of the two had once worked for Salise.

When I told Salise this and gave her the description of the man Madonna had given me, Salise knew exactly who it was. She'd had to dismiss the man a week before, and knew it was likely he was going to hold a grudge and try to get back at Salise by hurting her beloved animals. It is sad when human vindictiveness hurts animals.

I was very impressed with Madonna's intelligence. Her pictures were clear and her telepathic communication was detailed. She left nothing out. She told me there were two other adult pigs taken, which Salise confirmed. Madonna said the two pigs had squealed loudly and had been very difficult for the men to catch.

The truck was backed up to the pen. After the men ushered the squealing pigs into the truck, Madonna said the door had closed. She could see nothing, but sent me with her body telepathically that they had turned to the right after going down the drive, and then to the left I felt the swing in my body when the truck was going around the turns. Then they went left again. Then Madonna felt she was on a much busier road because she heard traffic.

I asked Madonna if she had gone a short way or a long way. She felt it was a long way along a busy road with many other cars. I felt they must have gone on a highway because that's the only place there would have been traffic at that time. By indicating with her body movement, Madonna told me they then took another left turn. She communicated with me through feelings and her body senses. I asked her if she could send me any pictures of where she was, but she was shut up in the dark, so there were no landmarks to guide our search.

I got an unpleasant feeling in my mouth, and knew Madonna didn't like the food she was being given. She told me they had given her some bread and that was all, so I knew she was hungry. Madonna was very concerned about what was going to happen to her and her babies.

At the time, I asked Salise not to release any of these details Madonna had given me to the press, because I was worried there would be a backlash against the sanctuary. People can sometimes be funny about the work I do. Salise had already paid a dear price with the loss of her pigs, and I didn't want anything more to happen to her or to the sanctuary.

Though I could not offer much hope for the recovery of her pigs, I explained to her that whatever happened, these people would not get away with the theft. The law of the universe says that what you give out you get back, so the men who caused Salise's heartache would have heartaches of their own to deal with one day.

Though I worked very closely with my guides, trying to find the pigs was almost an impossible task. I did not know how long the van had traveled or where it had gone on the freeway. Madonna had not been able to look out from the truck or see any landmarks. I felt very saddened. They was only a slight chance of getting the pigs back.

The good thing was that the press was covering the pignapping closely, so every few days there would be an update. The people who had stolen the pigs didn't think for a minute that the press would pick up this story. They were going to have difficulty getting rid of their captives.

During the course of the next week, I continued to pick up the pigs' energy. I also asked my guides to bring in some information on the physical level about the pigs' location, which they did. But we were no closer to finding Salise's pigs than we had been at the beginning. We all continued to pray, and many of my friends and clients were praying too.

Two weeks later Salise had a desperate call from a lady who had bought a baby pig from a pet shop. The woman said the pig was so small she didn't know how to feed it. She was afraid the piglet was dying. Salise told her to bring the pig to Special Pals, not knowing whether it was one of her pigs or not.

Salise and I stayed in contact over the phone. After I connected to the baby pig, I knew it was one of hers, but could not get any information on the rest of the family. Salise named the little pig Wilbur. She nursed him back to health, and he quickly became the darling of Special Pals. Even the other animals seemed to acknowledge that Wilbur was special.

Wilbur

Wilbur goes to the animal sanctuary each day, and at night, he stays with Mary Schweiger, a member of the Special Pals Board of Directors. He's wiggled his way into all our hearts and I see him regularly. He is a very superior pig; in fact, he doesn't believe he is a pig at all. Salise laughs whenever I say this, but I believe Wilbur was a nobleman in a former life, because he conducts himself with such dignity and strength of purpose.

Wilbur's greatest friend is a beautiful German shepherd named George who has appointed himself Wilbur's guardian. George sleeps on the bed with Wilbur at Mary's house every night. When they arrive at the sanctuary in the morning with Mary, George stands in front of Wilbur and protects him from the other dogs at the shelter, particularly new dogs who may not yet be aware of Wilbur's importance.

This happy state of affairs continued for a while. Whenever I went to visit Wilbur, the first thing I felt was a cold, wet nose pushing against my leg. When I sat down, he would jump right up my back and start nuzzling me with his strong nose as he squealed with joy.

Then one morning Salise called and left a frantic message on my answering machine saying Wilbur had been stolen again. She was absolutely devastated. I continued to let the answering machine play my messages as I tried to think of what to do. Before I could even formulate a plan of action, a new message from Salise informed me that Wilbur had been found. She was deliriously happy.

I phoned Salise straightaway and she proceeded to tell me about Wilbur's latest adventure, and what an adventure it was!

Mary had gotten up early that morning to take two dogs to the vet for minor surgical procedures. Normally, she fed all the animals together, but since the dogs would be undergoing anesthesia, they couldn't be fed. Though Wilbur was ravenous, she gave him only a dish of plain oats that she knew the dogs would ignore, to avoid problems of jealousy or hurt feelings. She planned to supplement the pig's oat snack with a full meal while the dogs were in surgery.

Naturally, Wilbur accompanied Mary and the two dogs to the vet. Though Wilbur didn't need veterinary attention, he liked to be included in all the outings. Mary loaded the three animals in the back of her pickup and started her journey. She arrived at the vet and went in with the two dogs, Wilbur following close on her heels. Mary told Wilbur to wait in the waiting room and not to move as she took the dogs for their treatment.

By this time, Wilbur was well past his accustomed breakfast time and his stomach was rumbley. So, being Wilbur and a very noble and self-determined pig (not to mention hungry), he opened the door of the clinic while the receptionist was otherwise occupied and went on his way.

Twenty minutes later Mary came out and found the waiting room empty . . . no Wilbur. The receptionist had no idea where he might have gone. Since Mary is a professional animal rescuer, she knew the first thing to do was call Animal Control and alert them to the fact that Wilbur was on the loose.

As it happened, Animal Control had just received an urgent call from a nearby country club saying they had a most unusual guest. A gentleman playing golf had been amazed at the speed with which Wilbur went sailing across the course to the clubhouse, following his strong sense of smell to the enticing aroma wafting from the buffet line in the main dining room. The hungry pig, after being treated to the best food any pig has ever been fed, decided he also wanted eggs for breakfast and where better to get them than a posh country club? His arrival in the dining room caused quite a stir, but to Wilbur it was perfectly normal as he was always in the dining room at Mary's house when her family ate, and in fact, often ate with them. He was used to having the best of everything.

Without waiting to be seated, Wilbur cut ahead of most of the guests in line and helped himself to the eggs and buttered toast in the buffet. He was quite a sight, standing on his hind legs in the buffet line, his snout pushed down into the breakfast entrees. Though the wait staff didn't quite know how to handle Wilbur, they were more amused than alarmed by his sudden appearance.

Soon though, the gig was up. Mary arrived looking a bit stern, ready to take Wilbur back to Special Pals. But the normally outgoing pig wouldn't look her in the eye. He knew he shouldn't have gone off like he did especially since he'd been stolen once before. He didn't mean to worry her, but he'd been hungry, and it wasn't every day a noble pig got a chance to dine with the finest members of Houston society.

Mary picked Wilbur up, but he hadn't finished his breakfast so he wasn't amenable to the idea of leaving yet. He squealed in protest. The dining staff indicated it was all right for Mary to put Wilbur down. The damage had already been done and what was another four eggs or so? Plus the guests seemed to be amused at the idea of a pig dining in their midst.

Mary put Wilbur down and he finished up the eggs. From then on, Mary learned not to delay Wilbur's mealtimes by even a few minutes, for fear that he would find a way to feed himself.

Sadly, since this adventure, Mary passed away in a tragic accident. Though I miss her terribly and the wonderful work she did for Special Pals, I know she is working even harder to help animals now that she has passed over. Wilbur and George especially miss her company, but Salise has given them a loving home at Special Pals.

Foxy

One early winter morning in 1995, I noticed a little black animal outside, lying down and scratching itself. At first, I thought it was Wellington, my cat, then realized he had too much common sense to be out in the cold and rain when he had a nice warm house to stay in. So I went downstairs and saw that it was a little black dog no bigger than my Wellington, in fact even a bit smaller than my well-fed feline.

I noticed the dog seemed frightened and cold, and was obviously hungry. She was very nervous as I approached, and ready to bolt, so I turned back toward my house, all the while sending the communication that everything was all right. I told her telepathically that she was not to worry or be scared, but should follow me back to my house where she would get a dish of food and a treat. As I got to my back door, I turned my head slightly and could see the little dog was following me, but very slowly because she was shivering so much that she had trouble walking.

I help many abandoned or lost dogs to find new homes, so I brought this one into my house as a matter of course. I gave her food and water right outside the back door, but every time I approached her, she backed off. She obviously did not want to come into a strange house. I walked away to give her time to get used to her new surroundings. Finally, I went back into the lounge and got down flat on my stomach on the floor so that I would appear to be on the same level with the dog, closer to her own size and therefore, less intimidating. This is a trick that works to calm most frightened animals.

She wanted to come into the house, but she was scared. She would walk up to the door, then back away. I decided to go upstairs and get a blanket to make a nest for the dog so she would at least have a warm and dry place to get into. I left the back door open a bit so the small dog could get inside. She was still dripping wet. I hoped she would climb into the bed I'd made for her and rest.

I came downstairs about a hour later and sure enough, there she was, all curled up in the bed resting. But when she heard me coming she looked at me and went to move outside again. I talked to her gently, reassuring her that she was safe. I lay down on my stomach again, stretched out my hand toward her and started transmitting to her that everything was fine; she could come in and she would be warm and safe with us. I assured her she wasn't going to be hurt, but she already seemed to know that.

The little dog scampered into the house with all the enthusiasm of the puppy that she was. She started running all around and shaking herself off, then she came up to me and let me pet her. I went to get a towel to dry the little dog off. I kept the door to the upstairs closed because of Bella and Wellington. I didn't want my other pets to frighten the little dog or to be frightened of her. I picked her up and toweled her until she was dry.

By this time the dog was beginning to feel a little bit more at home, so I let her come upstairs to meet Bella, Fitz, Emma, and Wellington. I named the dog Foxy because she looked just like a black fox. Though I was a bit worried about jealousy at first, my beloved Rhodesian Ridgeback, Bella, loved the little dog and was happy to have her with us. Fitz and Emma just rolled their eyes, but have been as taken as I with Foxy. Fitz now affectionately calls her "the little monster." My cat, Wellington, was of course, unmoved, believing the existing balance of one cat and one dog was the correct one. But he too has since been turned around by our charming black pup.

Foxy wanted to play with everyone, but the older animals were not amused. Bella was more curious than anything else. Wellington was most disgusted and asked me, "What's this thing coming in here?"

I tried to find Foxy's owner by advertising in the paper, but no one came forward. I looked everywhere to see if anyone had put any posters out, but had no luck. So I decided to find a new home for Foxy. Unfortunately, the pup wasn't house-trained. Before I could find a new home for her, I had to get Foxy trained.

I knew the small dog had been traumatized because I could not get her to communicate. Animals that have been badly treated sometimes do not speak for two to three weeks after arriving in a new home. I wanted to find out more about Foxy, so I decided to work through Bella, because the little dog had begun to make herself at home and become friends with Bella.

I heard of a lady who had lost her dog, but she was traveling and wouldn't be back for another few days. I had another homeless dog due to arrive that evening so I didn't have much time to make arrangements for Foxy. Lois, one of the animal foster parents I work with regularly, said she would be happy to foster Foxy for a few days to make room in my house for the other little stray dog that had been found wandering alongside a road with no tag.

The day came when Foxy would have to go. Though she had spent the week destroying my house, chewing up everything and making messes everywhere, she had already managed to worm her way into the hearts of everyone in my home.

I could see that Bella was sad to learn Foxy was going. She had found a little friend she really liked and now that friend was leaving. I explained we had to do this so we could help another little lost dog. I put Foxy in the car and drove her to Lois's office. Lois was expected shortly, and the secretary said I could leave Foxy with her until Lois arrived. I had another appointment so I had no choice but to leave her with the secretary. I felt relieved because the girl was a great dog lover and immediately put Foxy on her knee and cuddled her while she answered the telephone. I felt quite comfortable that Foxy was in good hands.

The day passed very quickly as I was busy with animals and clients. When I saw that it was almost three, I decided to call Lois to see how our little orphan was. To my horror, Lois told me Foxy had gotten out of the office when some clients came in. By the time I got there, the entire office was looking for Foxy. She'd been sighted but every time anyone got close, she would run away. It was getting cold and dark, and I was feeling frantic. I felt so bad about Foxy being lost again so soon after I had found her.

Charlotte, Lois's secretary, was driving around praying to find Foxy. Finally, she spotted the little dog about two miles away from the office, running across a very busy road. Charlotte said Foxy just darted across through the traffic. I think she must have borrowed a few of Wellington's nine lives that day. Charlotte tried to call Foxy but she wouldn't come because she was too afraid. I quickly went with Lois and we followed Charlotte to the last spot where Foxy had been seen and started to call her name. I was worried because Foxy had had her new name for only a week, and still didn't respond reliably to a summons. I called and called, feeling quite distraught. I couldn't bear the thought of Foxy being lost once and then within a week being lost again. She was such a little soul, frightened and bewildered.

Sometimes it is difficult to trust my instincts when I am emotionally involved in a case. I was very emotionally involved with

Foxy, and knew I had to relax if I was going to help her. We'd been looking for almost five hours, but I decided to give it another half hour. By this time, it was nearly dark and getting bitterly cold. I walked deeper into the woods by the side of the road and shouted Foxy's name at the top of my lungs, but to no avail. I was really panicking. I prayed for Foxy to please hear my voice. As I walked back to Lois and Charlotte who were also calling Foxy, I happened to look behind me and there, running at about a hundred miles an hour, was this little black ball of fur. She jumped straight up into my arms and I was overjoyed. I found myself sitting on the ground sobbing with joy.

Foxy was licking me all over and for the first time she communicated. I heard her say, "I knew you would come for me!" That's what really broke my heart. I explained that I'd had to leave her and she understood. I told her I would take her home and keep her a bit longer until I could find her a new home. I reasoned that maybe it was for the best because Foxy was still not completely house-trained. When I called Fitz and asked to bring her back, he was so upset he said, "You must bring her back immediately." I think he had already fallen in love with her.

When I brought her home that evening, Foxy had quite a reception from Bella and even old Wellington, but nothing like what Foxy got from Fitz. We told ourselves it was only temporary, that we'd give her a lot more love just until we could find her a permanent home. But even then, I think I knew we could never give her up for adoption again.

When I took her to the vet to get her shots the next day, he said she was only six to seven months old, and a fine specimen of a breed I was not familiar with, a Schipperke, or Dutch Captain's Boat Dog. The vet said he knew somebody who would love to have Foxy for breeding purposes, and he assured us the family would provide a very good home for the dog. Fitz and I looked at each other and said almost together, "No, she's not ready to go yet!" (I'm sure we'll still be saying that in ten years time.)

That evening Bella told me that Foxy had had a very sad life. Foxy still couldn't communicate well because she was so confused and upset, but Bella was able to make out more of what she was saying than I could. Bella then transmitted to me what Foxy had told her. Bella told me that Foxy's mummy (meaning her human mom) threw her into the street, and she had walked her feet raw looking for a new home. She'd been kept in a cage in the backyard by her unfeeling first owners, who never talked to her, which made her very sad. Foxy missed her dog mummy very much, because she was so young when she was taken away from her.

While Bella was still alive, there was just enough room in our four-poster bed for all of us, since Bella was rather large and took up a lot of space. I got used to sleeping with Bella on one side and Foxy on the other. In quite a determined fashion, she had stolen all our hearts.

Foxy brought joy into all our lives, but especially to Bella, who enjoyed having a canine companion in the last months of her life

Kiwi

My friend Helen Stroud called to tell me that one of her cats, Kiwi, was missing. Kiwi was so named because Helen's youngest child had trouble pronouncing "Kitty." It came out "Kiwi" instead.

I first met Helen when she called me to do some healing on Kiwi. The cat had had a rather dramatic start in life. Shortly after Helen and her family found the abandoned kitten, our area suffered a devastating flood. Helen's family and pets survived the trauma of rising water together, but after the flood, Kiwi had fallen ill.

Kiwi's illness was due as much to stress and trauma as anything else. After I sent her some healing energy, she bounced right back and had been fine ever since. Now she was lost, and Helen, like most people whose pets have gone missing, was frantic. She had searched the neighborhood with no luck, and her children were absolutely devastated.

I connected to Kiwi's energy and got the feeling the cat wasn't too far away, perhaps right in Helen's yard. But she wasn't lost at all; she was hiding out by choice. I asked Kiwi for a description of her location and she sent me a picture of flat gray rocks stacked up, with soil behind them. She said the steps to the house were nearby though she couldn't tell me whether it was the front or back of the house as animals make no such distinctions. She also sent me a picture of a very large, dense shrub, and I sensed that this was where she was hiding, under the shrub in Helen's garden. I relayed this information to Helen and she told me she had a rock border around a garden near her front door. She went and looked for Kiwi there, and called and called, but caught no glimpse of her pet. Still, I knew this was where the cat was hiding out, so I told Helen to put out food and water for her pet.

I suggested that if Helen would give her a day or two, Kiwi would probably calm down and come home on her own. But even as I said it, I could feel Kiwi clamoring to communicate, so I asked why she was camped out in the garden, hiding from her loving family. When I asked the cat what was wrong, she poured out a tale of jealousy and intrigue.

Kiwi told me there was another cat in the household, Annabel, who was the favorite of Helen's husband, Dan. Because of this lofty position, Annabel lorded it over the other cats in the house and was quite mean to Kiwi. When I connected to Annabel, she told me she thought Kiwi's skittishness was foolish, and made fun of the nervous cat whenever the opportunity presented itself. And she was always rubbing Kiwi's nose in the fact that the master preferred her over Kiwi.

Just that morning, Annabel had hissed and spit at Kiwi, and tried to slash her across the nose. When Dan heard the commotion, he scolded Kiwi, but not Annabel, which had sorely wounded Kiwi's feelings. On top of all this, Helen's house was full of commotion because she and Dan were preparing for a holiday party that evening. Kiwi overheard Dan asking that all the pets be put out before the guests arrived. The beautiful gray cat had had enough. She decided to put herself out, permanently. She was determined to see her plan through, but she was also very scared.

As Kiwi and I communicated, Helen's other cats came through. As Kiwi had mentioned, Annabel was imperious, and very proud of her position as the master's favorite. Surprisingly though, Annabel was not the only cat in Helen's household who was exasperated with Kiwi. "She's too nervous," they all chorused. "She won't come down when guests are here and is always hiding in the cupboard, which is silly, because Helen and her children are very kind to us."

I discovered all the cats had been in the flood together. They had willingly tolerated Kiwi's skittishness for a few months after the catastrophe, but now they were out of patience with her.

This was going to be a complex case. Just as we get along better with some people than others, so do animals form intricate social communities based on a spirit of mutual cooperation. If one dog or cat or bird or hamster or horse doesn't fit in, then that animal will be shunned by the others. This apparently was what had happened to Kiwi. No wonder she wanted to leave.

Two days after Kiwi's disappearance, Helen went shopping. As she turned into her driveway, she thought she caught a glimpse of Kiwi as she bounded across the lawn into the front garden. But by the time Helen parked her car and ran back, there was no trace of the cat.

I connected to Kiwi again and she told me the other cats in the house had told her to stop being silly and come back inside. "But I am too scared," Kiwi told me. "There are a lot of wheels going by and noise, and I don't want to move from this safe place."

Now that Helen knew Kiwi was in the front garden, she had taken to leaving her front door open during the day, hoping the frightened cat would see it and dash inside. She had the door propped open with a large can of peas. Kiwi sent me a picture of the door with the canned peas next to it, but she still had no intention of leaving her sanctuary.

Helen had me tell Kiwi that she would leave open the door of a stone potting shed that connected to the house in the rear. I told Kiwi if she waited until it was dark, she could sneak around the house, go through the shed and right up the back stairway. But Kiwi was beginning to enjoy her new home. She could watch the birds and small animals, and didn't have to endure the taunts of her fellow felines. Kiwi loved Helen and her children very much, but would not go back inside the house because of the situation with the other cats. Helen left food outdoors for a number of months without ever seeing Kiwi, and provided a warm shelter. At first the other cats felt odd about Kiwi being out in the garden, but eventually everyone got used to the situation.

I must say, in the years I have been helping to recover lost animals, I have never had a story with such an unusual conclusion. Kiwi moved outdoors in December of 1994, and lived there several months. Then one day when I tried to connect to her energy, it wasn't there anymore, and I knew she had passed over. Helen was very sad when I told her the news, but knows that Kiwi has gone to a much better place.

MOST lost pet stories do not have happy conclusions. It is best to do everything in your power to prevent your pet from becoming lost in the first place. You must be vigilant about his safety and make sure he has a secure place to stay, especially if he is spending long hours unsupervised outdoors. Make sure your animal is wearing proper ID tags with its name and your phone number displayed. If your dog or cat has a tendency to lose collars, secure the ID tags to a body harness. Otherwise, whoever finds your dog or cat has no way of knowing who the animal belongs to. They will either adopt your pet themselves, or take it to an animal shelter, where it stands a very good chance of being killed. Either way, you won't see your pet again.

If your pet is lost, remember to contact the Humane Society or animal shelter in your area immediately. Most shelters recommend visiting every three days. I say go EVERY day. You could lose your pet otherwise, as animal shelters in this country are chronically overcrowded and deal with this problem by killing most of the animals brought to them, healthy or not.

Put up posters with your pet's picture in the area where they disappeared. Remember that lost animals tend to stay on the move because they are looking for their home. Dogs can cover ten to fifteen miles a day in their search, and cats hitch rides in service vehicles, so don't confine your search to the few blocks around your home, but work outward as the days go by, to keep up with your pet's possible progress. I have recovered animals as far as fifty miles away from their original location.

Perhaps nowhere is the old cliché, "An ounce of prevention is worth a pound of cure," more true than in pet ownership. If you are a diligent and responsible pet owner, you reduce the chance that you will ever have to deal with the heartbreak of a lost pet.

ONE of the most fascinating things about pets is their diverse personalities. It has been no surprise to me as I become more and more involved in animal communication, to discover our pets find us just as fascinating as we find them. You may think no one is around, but your pet is watching you. I share some funny human stories I've been told by animals in the next chapter.

CHAPTER ELEVEN

What the Butler Saw

Your Pet Is Watching You

*T*he idea that pets are acute observers of human behavior is disconcerting to some people. But animals have no malice in them, and the stories they tell on their owners, no matter how embarrassing, are relayed in all innocence.

Think of how you delight in watching your pet, how you enjoy entertaining your friends with stories of his exploits. Does it not make sense that animals would enjoy the same thing, swapping stories of their owners back and forth?

You'll recall from the first chapter of this book that as a child in Hartwell, England, I was privy to every secret in our village, courtesy of my inquisitive animal friends. Trying to determine the source of my intelligence regularly confounded my parents. The truth that I told them, that my animal friends had given me all the gossip, was a truth they simply could not comprehend.

Animals in a neighborhood often trade stories about what is going on with their owners' families, and how their owners treat them. My client Nancy saw her dog take a piece of chicken she had just been given and carry it in her mouth to the dog next door, who was neglected by its owners and often went unfed. I know the poor hungry dog had telepathically sent a message to Nancy's dog, saying it hadn't been fed and was hungry, and could she spare a bit of that nice chicken it was smelling? Nancy's dog was generous and kindhearted, and so well taken care of by Nancy that it didn't mind sharing. But remember that animals have different personalities just as we humans do. Another dog may not have been so willing to share.

Both domesticated and wild animals communicate with each other and are likely to exchange information and warnings. For example, when my friend Pat showed herself sympathetic to wild life, she experienced a positive invasion of furry creatures in her large and heavily wooded backyard. Pat and I know it was because the animals had telepathically transmitted a message throughout the wood saying she was a kind and friendly human. Actually, many of the animals were probably already in residence, but didn't feel emboldened to show themselves until they were certain it was safe.

I'm sure many of you have seen homes where cats seem to congregate. You can be sure when you see such a house that the cats have been telling each other there was a feline-loving human in residence at that address. I've been told that sick raccoons present themselves regularly at the animal shelter here in Montgomery County. It is because they know that is where they can get help and volunteers at the animal shelter are constantly putting out the pictures and feelings of helping animals. Animals in the area surrounding the shelter receive these pictures telepathically. They feel the positive energy coming from the shelter, so they use their senses as a sort of built-in compass to find help.

Though wild animals certainly watch us with the same interest that our pets do, the funniest stories I've been told about humans come to me from domesticated pets. Since these stories are potentially embarrassing, I've left out the names of the humans involved, and changed the names and identifying characteristics of the pets. So if you think you recognize yourself here, it's just coincidental.

Dabney and Eliza

A couple came to consult me because their two Golden Retrievers, Dabney and Eliza, were getting out of the bedroom each night and wrecking the house. Just that morning they had awakened to discover the corner of the coffee table chewed, cushions torn from the sofa, and a vase of flowers knocked over and broken. They asked me to find out why their dogs wouldn't stay in the bedroom with them at night as they were instructed to do, and why they were so destructive.

The answer to the destruction was easy. When animals are bored and unsupervised, they often go on rampages that result in severe damage to clothing, furniture, and knickknacks. They don't see it as naughty; to them it is simply play.

When I connected to the two dogs, I found them quite affable. I asked why they wouldn't stay in the bedroom. Before they could reply, I began to experience quite an unpleasant sensation in my nose. Although the dogs knew their owners were upset with their disobedience, they transmitted with pictures and feelings the clear message that they simply could not stay in that bedroom. I wondered if their desire to escape was related to the sudden sensitivity in my nose.

Nonetheless, I was quite stern with the dogs. "You know you must stay in the bedroom," I told them.

"But we can't!" came the plaintive answer.

I knew there was more to it than they were telling me. After quite a bit of prodding, I discovered their human father had a chronic case of nocturnal intestinal gas and the dogs' noses were quite sensitive to this. Things were fine for the first thirty minutes or so after the humans lay down in the bed. The dogs behaved nicely and everyone fell asleep. But once the nightly flatulence started, they felt compelled to escape the room quickly, an escape made possible by Dabney's clever turning of the L-shaped handle on the bedroom door.

Not wishing to cause my clients embarrassment, I simply told them that the dogs had requested their own bedroom, which they had not, and asked if they had another room the dogs could sleep in. Since the couple's children were grown and they lived in a large house, the request was simple to fulfill. I suggested they fill the selected room with toys and chewies to keep their playful pets occupied and out of trouble. I also hinted that they might find it wise to change the style of the door handle in that room, to keep Dabney from effecting an escape.

Once the retrievers were moved into their own room full of interesting toys, and not subjected every night to the noxious smells produced by their father, the owners informed me that the midnight rampages stopped and all was peaceful once more in their home.

Still, I can't help but wonder how the man's wife slept through all that. Perhaps she was blessed with a poor sense of smell, or maybe she slept with a nose plug.

Teddy and Matilda

One day, I was consulted by a lady who told me that she and her husband were distraught because their two seven-year-old purebred cats were suddenly having accidents all over the house: on the sofa, on the rug, even on the bed. The problem was particularly puzzling because the cats had always been perfectly behaved. The husband was so angry about their ruined carpet and furniture that he told his wife she must correct the problem immediately or get rid of the cats. There would be no compromise. (It will perhaps give you some insight into this man's character that he decided his wife alone had to solve their joint problem, and that insight may help explain his wife's behavior later in this story.)

He seemed to be the sort of man who loved his wife and cats well, as long as they did just as he wanted them do. But any deviation from his program was excuse enough to get rid of the cats. Perhaps his wife felt her position was tenuous as well. As you shall soon see, the problem really was more the wife's than the husband's.

The couple lived in a Southern colonial mansion in one of the most elegant areas of Houston. Their home was filled with priceless antiques and artifacts, prized possessions the cats were eliminating, one by one. The lady begged for my help. She loved her cats and did not want them to be put away for the sake of a piece of furniture.

When I connected to her two cats, they immediately assured me that they loved their "mummy and daddy" (as animals often refer to their owners), but really didn't like that new man mummy had started bringing home in the afternoon.

I realized immediately the lady had taken a lover. Just that quickly, I'd discovered the answer to the puzzle, the obvious source of the cats' upset.

I decided to get a bit more information from the cats, and invited them to continue their story. They went on to complain that their "mummy" had the nerve to pitch them out of their bedroom, the one they had always shared with their owners, and then she closed the door, shutting them out. Feeling neglected and somewhat put out by this lack of regard for their rights, they responded in the time-honored tradition of scorned pets everywhere: They started making messes all over the house. They deliberately picked the most open and obvious spots to deposit their "accidents," which were no accident at all, to let their owners know how displeased they were with the recent turn of events.

The lady must have noticed my amused look and realized something was wrong. I told her what the cats had just relayed to me, and then it was her turn to be surprised.

"I can't believe they knew I had taken a lover," she said.

"They know everything," I told her.

"But what shall I tell my husband?" she asked.

I informed her I didn't give that sort of advice; all I could do was tell her how to deal with her cats. But I did suggest that perhaps it would be wiser to meet her lover elsewhere, to avoid upsetting the cats. I felt that alone would restore tranquillity to the domestic life of her cats. How to restore tranquillity to the domestic life of the woman was another matter entirely.

The woman left my studio in something of a state, and I knew I would never see her again. But I am sure she never thought when she brought her lover home it would affect her cats so dramatically, or that they would soon be telling her deepest secret to me.

Buster

A client came to my office very concerned because her eight-year-old Border collie's coat was falling out. There hadn't been a change in Buster's diet; he didn't have fleas or a skin inflammation. Her vet had thoroughly examined the dog and could find nothing wrong.

When I tuned in to Buster, I discovered a very cheerful dog

who told me he knew his mummy was coming to see me, and had been waiting for me to speak to him. Buster even told me why his mummy was consulting me; she was worried about his coat. Then he told me his hair was falling out just like his daddy's. This gave me my first clue to the problem.

I asked the lady if her husband was experiencing hair loss. She answered immediately that he was absolutely obsessive about his receding hairline.

"He stands in front of the mirror and stares at his hair for fifteen minutes every morning," she told me, "then asks me if I think any more has fallen out overnight. He's very worried about it."

I asked her if Buster ever went into the dressing room with his daddy while these conversations were going on. She told me the dog always accompanied her husband during his morning routine. Buster sent me a picture of his daddy working out on an exercise machine, then going into the shower. He told me this was his favorite part of the morning, because he loved getting a spray of water in his face. He said his daddy was very particular about his dress, sometimes changing shirts twice in the morning if he didn't like the way he looked.

My client confirmed that her husband was very fastidious, and was stunned when I told her Buster knew she was sad over losing one of her favorite blue earrings. The chatty dog also mentioned that he much preferred her new bed covering to the old one and wanted to know for certain if she was going to keep it. She couldn't believe her pet was so observant, but we were finding that Buster really had an eye for detail.

I picked up a feeling of extreme worry from Buster. He told me his daddy was very worried because his hair was falling out, and now his mommy was upset because his hair was beginning to fall out too.

There was a definite connection between the two problems. Buster had picked up his owner's fear of hair loss. Because he loved his owner so much and strongly identified with him, he started worrying his hair would fall out too. His worry had grown so all-consuming it became a self-fulfilling prophecy and Buster started to experience a sort of sympathetic baldness, shedding so much hair that he too developed bald spots.

Buster asked me if his hair would keep falling out like his daddy's. I promptly told him that dog hair did not fall out like human hair, so he had no need to worry. I told his mommy that Buster was picking up tremendous stress and worry from his daddy. His belief that he would become bald like his daddy was so powerful that it was actually making his hair fall out, even though there was no physical reason for the hair loss.

I told my client she had to constantly remind Buster his hair was not supposed to fall out so he needn't worry about such a thing happening. I explained to Buster that his master's worry about his inevitable baldness was natural, but that didn't mean that Buster's hair would fall out too.

I asked the lady to keep me informed of Buster's condition and to tell me if there was any change in his coat. I told her to reinforce the idea that his hair was fine; it was only Daddy's hair that was falling out.

My client returned a month later to tell me that Buster's hair was growing back, and all the bald patches were covered over. If only I had the same luck in restoring human hair, I should be able to retire in six months!

IT is not necessary to go around in a state because you know your pet is watching you. Rather, let it serve as a reminder to be on your best behavior; to be the best possible pet owner you can be. If you are kind and loving to your pet, and treat him with courtesy and respect for his feelings, then you really have nothing to worry about, because your pet will have only nice things to say about you. If occasionally your pet lets you know with a look that he has caught you in a funny situation, let it go. None of us is perfect.

But you shouldn't have to guess at your pet's thoughts and feelings. With a bit of practice, almost anyone who is open to the idea can learn how to communicate telepathically with animals. In the next chapter, I will give you step-by-step instructions on how to achieve that communication, along with easy exercises you can do to test your ability to reach your pet on the telepathic level. You can build a better relationship with your animal if you just open your mind.

CHAPTER TWELVE

If I Could Talk to the Animals

Communicating with Your Animal

*M*y clients often ask me exactly how I communicate with their pets. But what people are really curious about is whether they themselves can establish telepathic communication with animals. The answer is yes. In this chapter, I will explain the specifics of telepathic communication, which is how I "talk" to animals, and give step-by-step instructions that will enable many readers to open a channel of telepathic communication with their own pets.

The most important skill you must master before you attempt telepathic communication with your pet is the art of relaxation. Many people find it difficult to meditate or relax. If you follow these basic instructions, you can achieve a state of relaxation rather quickly. Unplug the phone, turn off the television and radio, lock the door if you have to. If there is a particular piece of soft music you like, listen to that. I like to be still and quiet with no music. You will find what works best for you.

Sit on a comfortable chair or lie on your bed and close your eyes. Concentrate on your breathing and breathe deeply in and out. Bring your awareness to your body. Start to relax your toes and feet. Feel the relaxed feeling traveling through your legs and knees up to the top of your legs as you continue to breathe deeply in and out. Feel the lower half of your body relaxing. Feel the relaxed feeling traveling through to your chest right through to your shoulders, then down through your arms and elbows to your wrists. Feel your hands and fingers relaxing. Feel that relaxation traveling up through your neck and face, relaxing your eyes. Soon your eyes will begin to feel heavy and now your head will be completely relaxed. Feel that wonderful feeling traveling throughout your body. Now that you are in a relaxed state, you are ready to start.

No matter how relaxed you are, you will not be successful if your pet is distracted. Animals will not listen if they have other things occupying their attention. Humans are not so different. If you were studying for an exam, your mind would be occupied with your work and not particularly receptive to any other stimuli. You would certainly not want to start a conversation. You would not even be listening.

It is the same with animals, even though their method of communication is telepathic and not verbal. When people tell me their dog won't listen to them, my first thought is, "What is he doing when you are trying to talk to him?" If he is busy scratching or watching a squirrel through the window, he won't be very interested in anything you have to say; he is already pleasantly occupied.

If you hope to have any success communicating with your pet, either telepathically or verbally, you must wait until your animal is quiet and not distracted by anything else before you try communicating with him. Make sure your animal has been fed and taken out, and that all his physical needs have been met before you begin. Choose a quiet time and make sure you have your pet's complete attention. Don't worry if your pet is dozing; you can reach him on a telepathic level even if he is sleeping. Then take your pet to the quiet, peaceful spot you have chosen, relax, clear your mind, and begin.

Telepathic communication is not as hard as you might think. I have developed two easy exercises—one for dogs and one for cats—that will give you clear proof that you have reached your animals on a telepathic channel. It's a bit more complex when you try to determine whether or not you have received telepathic communication from your pet, because that involves trusting your imagination and intuition. But we shall come to that later. First, the exercises, which are different for dogs and cats, because our most popular domestic pets react best to different stimuli.

Communicating with Your Dog

Either touch your animal or say his or her name so he will know you want to communicate. Imagine you are going to take your dog out for a walk. (Don't perform this experiment if the weather won't permit a walk, because it is very important to fulfill with physical action what we promise our animals on the telepathic level, or else they will learn to distrust us.) Imagine how much fun a walk would be and picture the path you will take, and all the exciting sights and scents your dog might encounter along the way. See yourself running or walking alongside your dog, and feel the exhilarating sense of freedom and the joy of experiencing nature firsthand.

The more you let your feelings and imagination soar, the stronger your communication will be and the better your chance of success. Be confident. You are painting pictures with your feelings and imagination, which your pet will see as surely as if you had painted them with a brush on canvas. Remember how you use your imagination in everyday life to create ideas and dreams, to set goals, and make plans. That is no different than what I am asking you to do with your pet.

Now, take the pictures and feelings you have created, and use your mind energy to "toss" them out as you would a ball from your hand. Then watch carefully to see your pet's reaction. If he starts to bark and runs excitedly to where his leash is kept, he has telepathically received the message that you want to take him for a walk, and now it is time to keep your promise. It really is that easy.

Communicating with Your Cat

Since a walk on a leash is not at all appealing to most cats, I've devised a different exercise for them. I suggest you entice cats with a treat. Picture yourself opening a can of his favorite food: tuna or chicken, whatever it is. Then imagine the tantalizing smell, the delicious taste. Send out the feelings of pleasure your cat will have when you share this treat with him, which will be soon if he shows you by his actions that he has received your message. If your cat starts meowing and rubbing himself against you, or showing you the behavior that typically precedes his mealtimes, then you will know you have succeeded.

IT is important to preserve the integrity of these experiments by using nothing other than the powers of silent suggestion on your pet. It's not fair to get out the leash or rattle the tuna can, because then the communication is auditory and not telepathic.

When you are attempting telepathic communication with your pet, it is also most important that your body and mind work together. Don't send one message with your mind and another with your physical body. That will confuse your animal and defeat your attempts to communicate. For instance, if you are telling your dog verbally (with your physical body) you want him to be nice to your new cat, but your mental image is of your dog chasing the cat, he is likely to act on the more powerful telepathic picture. Be sure to picture telepathically just what you want while you are saying it verbally.

Don't be too disappointed if you do not achieve success the first time you try these tests. Several factors can affect the outcome. If you are not relaxed, calm and focused, your telepathic communication may not be very clear. Remember too that animals vary in their ability and desire to communicate telepathically. If they are preoccupied with something else when you try these experiments, your pets will not pay much attention to you, novel though your communication attempts may be.

It is my belief that humans are all born with the ability to communicate telepathically. I also believe that if we didn't have the faculty of speech we would all communicate telepathically just as animals do. Everything we need for telepathic communication is already wired into our brains. But our lives are so busy and noisy; we are so preoccupied with our thoughts and the cares of our everyday lives that we don't take the time we need to be quiet and get in touch with our inner senses and our imagination, which are essential steps to access the telepathic channel.

As children, we are very aware of our inner senses. We trust our feelings and imaginations implicitly. Ideally, we should continue to trust our imagination as adults, but all too often we discount information that comes from our imagination, and tell ourselves it must not be real. But in order to communicate telepathically with our animals, we must believe in the power of our imaginations and not discount what we are sensing, feeling and hearing. Those feelings, ideas, thoughts, and pictures that come to us unbidden when we are relaxed and quiet are actually our animals' way of talking to us. If we shove them away, we are blocking a higher level of communication with our pets that could bring us even closer to them.

Remember how I told you earlier in this chapter that it was a bit more difficult to determine when an animal has sent a telepathic communication back to us? There is no sure-fire test for this. One of the most important things I tell my clients who are trying to establish telepathic communication with their animals is that they must not dismiss any thought, idea, or feeling that comes to them during their attempts to communicate telepathically with their pets, no matter how fantastic it may seem. Rather, they should learn to welcome the images and ideas that start flowing to them telepathically, because they contain valuable information that could give them deep insight into their pet's behavior and personality.

But what exactly is it you are looking for? If you have sent a telepathic communication to your pet, then suddenly discover an unusual idea or picture forming in your brain, or hear a response spoken inside your head, you have succeeded. Trust your imagination and do not dismiss these unfamiliar images and feelings out of hand. As you become more adept at telepathic communication, you will experience a whole new dimension of joy and awareness and gain an understanding of the animal kingdom that will enhance both your life and that of your animals.

My friend Pat, never had any experience with telepathic communication, but as she grew in awareness, she decided to try her hand at it and sent out a picture of a can of tuna to her cat, who was sleeping across the room. Pat concentrated on sending the delicious taste of the tuna, and the feeling of happiness the cat would have while eating the treat. Immediately, the cat woke

Seven Simple Steps to Communicating with Your Pet

ᔡ

1. Begin with a calm and tranquil mind and seek out a calm and tranquil atmosphere for you and your animal.

2. Say your animal's name telepathically to get its attention.

3. Visualize your animal as you say its name.

4. Send a picture of its physical body. Direct this to it, along with its name.

5. Ask if there is anything your pet would like you to do for it. Imagine your animal is sending an answer back to you and accept whatever you receive in your imagination.

6. Always acknowledge the answer, whatever you receive back from your animal.

7. Continue to ask it other questions, and remember to trust your imagination for what you are receiving back from your animal.

up, bounded across the room and up into Pat's lap, meowing loudly for the promised treat. Pat was quite taken aback with her quick success.

But don't worry if you don't receive an answer the first few times you communicate. It is a surprise to your pet the first time he hears your telepathic voice and some pets take a while to get used to hearing you on that channel. If you continue to practice, you will eventually succeed.

Keep your sessions brief, about ten minutes or so, as animals have short attention spans and tire quickly. If you drone on, you will lose their attention. Be aware of his body language, as that will give you clear signals about your pet's receptiveness.

Don't keep asking the same question for too long because animals get bored just like people do. If you don't receive an answer, change your question to something else. Try asking if there is anything your pet would like you to do for them. Give them a chance to think about your question. Don't ask more than one question at a time. Accept whatever you receive back, but don't add your thoughts to this feeling or picture. Always acknowledge your animal has spoken to you. Pet him, thank him and tell him how much you love him.

As your communication skills start to improve, you will find that you no longer have to meditate down. You will find you can use telepathic communication in your everyday life while going about your routine. If you are in your kitchen and have your pets' dinner ready or a treat for them, send the message out telepathically and see how they respond. Send a picture of the dinner and putting it down for them and them eating it. Try these little exercises as you go about your everyday routine and you will be pleasantly surprised to discover how your awareness and telepathic abilities are increasing.

When you have mastered the basics of telepathic communication, you can go a step further. Now you recognize your animal's language, your intuitiveness is sharpened, so therefore, you are using your energy and emotional body to its full capacity. You are not only speaking the animal's language, you are experiencing a whole new world of communication, and now you understand there is much more than the faculty of speech to communicate with. You are using your telepathic ability to communicate mentally, physically, and spiritually with your animal.

You will find once your physical body responds, you will start to feel and experience what the animal is feeling. Imagine yourself on all fours, in the same posture as your animal. Your arms are your pet's two front legs, your back legs are their back legs. Maybe you feel pain in your right leg. That would relate to your animal's right hind leg. If you get a pain in your left hand, that might mean your animal's left paw is hurting.

When you start to feel pain or uncomfortable feelings that you know do not relate to you, don't dismiss them. Your pet may be transmitting any discomfort he feels in his physical body to your physical body. This ability to communicate physical feelings telepathically will help you to know what is wrong with your animal before any veterinarian does. So now you are not only speaking with your mind energy, you are speaking with your emotional and physical body and your intuitiveness.

If you follow these basic steps of communicating with your animal, many of you will be able to establish a recognizable telepathic link with your pet. Once you are proficient, you will find you don't have to concentrate quite so hard on relaxing; it will begin to come automatically with practice.

If you hope to master telepathic communication, you must learn to trust your feelings and imagination as children do. You must be open so that the feelings and pictures your animals send to you are not discarded out of hand, but examined, interpreted, and utilized to enhance communication. Remember: Trust your imagination! With practice and concentration, many of you will be able to sign on to the telepathic communication channel your pets use every day.

Whether or not you ever experience telepathic communication with your animal, you can achieve much simply by making sure that all your spoken communications are delivered with love, gentleness and positive energy. In this way, your pet can always be assured of your love and caring, which will go a long way toward eliminating some common behavioral problems before they start.

How Animals Help People

We've talked quite a bit about different ways we can communicate with our animal companions, but now let's discuss how animals communicate with us. Animals want to help humans in any way they can. While all of us can benefit from having pets in our lives, perhaps no one loves and appreciates their furry friends more than people whose lives are restricted by advancing age, illness or disability. What frail seniors, sick and disabled people have in common is the isolation their condition imposes, and isolation leads to loneliness. Who better to alleviate loneliness than a warm and devoted animal that loves you unconditionally?

As you may well know from your own experience, animals have a special sensitivity to the needs of people who are experiencing any sort of difficulty. They seem to know instinctively just what is needed and do everything within their power to ease trying situations. They sense whenever we are not at our best and could use a little boost, and they cheerfully appoint themselves to provide that boost.

I frequently hear stories of animals that have spent the whole of a person's illness lying patiently on the foot of the bed, waiting for their human companion to recover from the flu or a cold or an injury. They also make themselves quietly available even if their human is not actually ill, but perhaps feeling just a little blue. If this has ever happened to you, you know what a great comfort it is to have your animal companion close at hand when you are not feeling your best. This is because animals are constantly transmitting out the feeling of love; when you pet or hold an animal you can feel the love from him. Love is the greatest pure healing energy in the universe. When humans who are not feeling well have contact with their pets, they receive the healing love energy from their animal companion and that is why they feel better.

Many people have asked me how animals know when we are feeling bad, particularly when we are trying to push and stay on our routine. It is because our comfortable and familiar scent changes when we fall ill, and our animal companions, who use their noses to gather information in much the same way that we use our eyes and ears, instantly know that something is off. Immediately, they make it their job to tend to us, sending us wave after wave of love. That is why having an animal around when we are ill actually makes us feel better. It's not just their physical presence that benefits us; it's the active healing they provide that helps us to mend from both physical and psychological distress.

Having animals around is also a wonderful effective remedy for stress. When you are feeling pressured and out of sorts, just a few minutes of cuddling and small talk with your beloved animal companion is often all it takes to get yourself feeling calm and centered once again.

But pets do more than just make us feel better; they can actually hasten our recovery and even improve our chances of surviving a life-threatening illness. If that sounds like a wild claim, let me assure you that it has been scientifically proven. Twenty-five years ago, Erika Friedmann, a researcher at the University of Pennsylvania, conducted a now-famous study on survival rates following a heart attack. Much to her own amazement and that of her colleagues, she discovered the most positive indicator of survival was pet ownership. In other words, if a person had a companion animal, they were much less likely to pass away in the year following their heart attack than people who did not have animals in their homes. In fact, so powerful is the love of our pets that studies have proven that people who do not have pets are five times more likely to die following a heart attack than people who do have animal companions.

How can this be? It is simple. Illness is a huge stress on the body, and as stress starts to build, it can trigger a cascade of detrimental side effects in the body, some of them potentially fatal. But animals, who are aware of everything, instinctively know when their human companion is in difficulty and insofar as they are able, they make it their job to protect them from further harm.

People often get angry and frustrated because they do not understand everything that has happened to them during an illness; yet, when they receive their animal's love it does make them feel better. They recover more rapidly and live longer because the energy of the love that their animal companion is projecting toward them acts as a healing blanket, shielding and protecting them from further harm.

Other studies have shown that having animals in your home reduces loneliness, promotes relaxation, lowers blood pressure and pulse rate and also helps to fight depression. You would have to swallow whole bottles of pills every day just to equal all the physical benefits that our animal companions provide, not to mention the psychological benefits. And for those of you who might be thinking that you do not need an animal friend because you have plenty of human ones, let me ask you this: Do all your human friends love you unconditionally? Because your animal friends do. It is the only kind of love they know how to give.

There are some cats that transmit healing energy that will sense when their human parent is ill by lying on their body, often on the chest area. Such cats are very aware and know that they have the ability to heal. The ancient Egyptians were well aware that cats have this ability to heal and had healing cats in all their temples. If your cat attempts to lie on you, know that it is his way of sending you healing energy so that you will feel better. Try to relax and lie still and allow your cat to stay on your body as long as he wishes, for he will know when his work is done.

It is quite interesting to note that veterinary studies prove that loving human companionship produces the same beneficial effects on animals' health and longevity as their companionship does on ours. This only goes to prove the incredible power of the bond between humans and animals.

Animals transmit compassion and love to their human companions in much the same way that a radio tower sends messages out over the airwaves. They know everything that is happening around them; if they sense that something is off, they want to help. When they are able to help their families by providing healing energy and companionship during times of illness or stress, they feel the same pride that we do when we perform important work.

Just as we put on our best business suit before we go into an important meeting, animals who are doing healing work like to dress up to show that they are doing something special as well. They love to wear bandanas; it makes them feel very important. So, if your animal companion is lying faithfully on the bed of your sick child, remember to praise him for his devotion and reward him by thanking him and giving him a hug.

Once the positive effects of companionship with animals were scientifically proven, many nursing homes and long-term care facilities created visitation programs to provide the love and healing benefits of animals to people whose condition or circumstances precluded them having pets of their own. Trained companion animals especially selected for their sociability and easygoing temperaments are taken around by volunteers to visit shut-ins and other people who do not regularly have access to companion animals. Wherever it has been implemented, the animal visitation day quickly becomes a favorite of residents at facilities like retirement homes and homes for developmentally disabled individuals.

While most animals are only too happy to provide this service to humans, it is wise to remember that a few are not willing. I once counseled a woman who had been through a long illness. She was upset because her dog, a beautiful Border collie named Mildred, would no longer come sit on her bed to keep her company. She and Mildred had always been close companions, spending every possible moment together. When I spoke to Mildred, it turned out that the smell of the harsh chemical disinfectant being used in the sick room was offensive to her delicate nose. Once her family switched to a natural cleanser, Mildred returned to her sick human's side.

Sometimes though, the pet's problem is the odor emanating from the sick person and there is little you can do about that except to explain to them what is happening. Animal's noses and olfactory systems are so much more sensitive than ours that they can pick up odors and nuances of scent we don't even realize are on the air. As I mentioned earlier, animals like smells that are comfortable and familiar; they help to keep them oriented. So when a person falls ill and suddenly starts giving off an entirely different odor, it can be quite upsetting and disorienting for their animal companions.

There are excellent animal visitation programs all over the country so I will mention just a few here. You can go online and perform an Internet search to locate one near you. The College of Veterinary Medicine at the University of Tennessee sponsors H.A.B.I.T. or Human-Animal Bond of Tennessee. The group makes regular visits to nursing homes, assisted living centers, retirement and mental health centers, residential facilities for children with special needs and adult day cares. Dr. Earl Strimple of Washington, D.C.'s MacArthur Animal Hospital created a nationally recognized program called "People Animals Love" to send companion animals to comfort people in prisons and hospitals.

No matter what they are called—Visiting Pets, Therapy Pets, or Animal Assistants—their purpose is the same . . . to bring a little warmth and love and cheer to people who desperately need some comfort and reassurance.

The idea of employing animals to assist humans who have health or mobility problems has become so well-regarded that many colleges now offer courses of study in animal-assisted therapy and counseling. Instead of simply visiting people, some companion animals are now trained to provide invaluable assistance to people who otherwise might not be able to have any independence.

We are all familiar with seeing-eye dogs; those brilliant and attentive canine companions that allow blind people to safely enjoy some mobility. We see them on the street with their human companions, carefully guiding them around obstacles in their paths, and steering them away from danger. We even see them in places where dogs are not normally allowed, such as restaurants, theaters and public transportation. But most of us are not aware that many other animals, including ponies and monkeys, are now routinely trained to work as service animals.

Catholic Charities provides free service ponies to developmentally challenged children. A national organization called Personal Ponies does the same thing for disabled children throughout the country. UK Miniature Shetlands, naturally hardworking, patient and kind by temperament, are trained to provide gentle companionship for such children. Parents frequently report that children whose behavior was unmanageable calm right down once they receive their very own ponies. Others whose children were suffering from depressed spirits due to their conditions or chronic illness report that all signs of sadness departed once their pony came to live with them.

The ponies realize they are taking care of the child they are assigned to and they take their responsibilities seriously. Some disabled children, such as those suffering from autism, are quite bright, but are virtually prisoners of their conditions, shut off from human contact and unable to communicate in any discernable fashion. While humans frequently label such children as "stupid," ponies know the children are not stupid at all. They speak telepathically to the child and for the first time, the child has someone to understand him. They feel heard because the pony understands and answers in the same language.

I once had a client who came to see me about her dog and brought along her autistic son. When they arrived, I picked up the boy's thoughts quite strongly; he was very excited about a recent ride on a therapy pony and wanted to know if he could have a pony of his own. His mother was blown away by the fact that I knew her son had just been riding and I explained to her how her son was transmitting his thoughts telepathically in the same way that animals do. Most of us let go of our capacity for telepathic communication once we master the power of speech, but disabled individuals who cannot speak have no other language other than the telepathic one. That is why they connect so strongly with animals because to them, animals are the only ones who understand them.

Ponies are not the only working service animals. More than twenty years ago, a trained capuchin monkey was placed in the home of a paralyzed man to see if she could help him with his day-to-day tasks such as eating and opening mail. The experiment was so successful that the Paralyzed Veterans of America and the National Science Foundation both provided grants to study monkeys and see if they could truly be trained as service animals for quadriplegics. The results of the studies were positive and an organization called Helping Hands was created to train and provide service monkeys. More than seventy are now in the homes of people throughout America who suffer from paralysis or degenerative diseases that impair their ability to move about and care for themselves. The group lovingly trains and places an additional twelve monkeys each year, which are provided free of charge to those needing them. They only use humane training methods, no punishment, to reward the monkeys for the invaluable service they render. Unlike service dogs that live anywhere from eight to twelve years on average, service monkeys have a life span of thirty to forty years, so the same monkey is able to stay and help its human companion over the course of a lifetime.

I've shared just a few stories about the benefits of animal companionship and I'm sure you know of many more. If you want to help people whose circumstances deprive them of the chance to have an animal companion on a regular basis, please consider volunteering for a pet therapy program.

It is not only domestic pets that can benefit from telepathic communication with humans. In the next chapter, I will share some interesting stories of communication with wild animals.

CHAPTER THIRTEEN

Howls and Whispers

Communicating with Wild Animals

So far we have talked only of domestic pets, but it is also possible to communicate telepathically with wild animals. Though the vast majority of requests for my help concern family pets, I do have cases in my files where a client asked that I establish communication with a wild or feral animal to help them resolve some problem.

Pat's Raccoons

My friend Pat has provided me with my most fascinating and perhaps longest-running case of telepathic communication with wild animals. One evening in the fall of 1995, Pat and I were together and I noticed she looked very tired. When I asked her why, she replied she had been up most of the night before due to a series of awful noises coming from her attic: crashes, thumps, skittering and scratching. Pat didn't know what was causing the noise, but was afraid her home had been invaded by an army of rats or worse. Her children were even more scared than she was.

I asked if I could use Pat's energy to connect to the nocturnal invaders and immediately sensed her intruder was a raccoon, a young female. As winter was approaching, I knew the animal was looking for a place to keep warm, but I also knew that attics, with their asbestos insulation and electrical wiring, could be very dangerous places for wild animals.

The raccoon said she had been living in a hollow in Pat's backyard that had caved in during a period of heavy rain. Now, she was looking for a new home. I asked how she had gained access to Pat's house and she told me there was a rotten place in the wood next to Pat's chimney and she had managed to chew through to the attic. The raccoon told me she could feel the warm air coming through the hole and decided Pat's attic would make a highly suitable winter home.

I told Pat to speak to the raccoon and tell her she must come out of the attic, but I knew she also had to provide the raccoon with an alternate home for the winter or the animal would not leave. She made that much very clear to me when I communicated with her. You must remember when you move wild animals from one place to another that you have to provide a suitable habitat for them to move into; otherwise you will have no luck with the transfer.

Though a bit skeptical, that evening Pat took a flashlight, shone it into the hole in her soffit, and told the raccoon she must speak to her. To Pat's surprise, the raccoon immediately came out and listened attentively while Pat told her she was welcome on her property, but that she must move to the new house she would provide. She even posed for a picture Pat took to show me. In the meantime, Pat asked the raccoon to quiet down at night, so that she and her children could sleep without interruption. Pat told the raccoon that if she had work to do, she should do it in the early evening, before her family went to sleep.

The raccoon turned and went back into the house. Immediately a commotion broke out and for the next three hours, the raccoon was busy in the attic. Suddenly, all became quiet, and remained quiet all night long. The raccoon kept to this pattern of work in the early evening and quiet all night. Pat decided this arrangement would be satisfactory, and so she lived all during the winter, with no difficulties from her resident raccoon and no disturbances. She left the hole in the soffit open for the raccoon to come and go.

Considering what happened to Pat and the raccoon the following spring, we now know it would have been better for Pat to have built the raccoon house at this time. But she really did not yet know enough about raccoons to design an effective home for them, plus she had some financial considerations that would not have permitted the construction of a suitable habitat at that time.

In the spring of 1996, two rogue male raccoons showed up to court Pat's boarder. Peace and quiet disappeared. I tried communicating with the two males to tell them they must quiet down, but they were in no mood to listen. Their emotions were high, and just as with humans, raging emotions kept the raccoons from choosing the best path. Their jealousy toward one another and fierce desire to prevail in the mating contest kept them from responding to my reasonable requests to stop being so loud and combative. Pat was falling over with fatigue and her children didn't want to stay at the house because of the noises the raccoons were making all night long.

Finally, one night while Pat and her children were watching television together, a furious fight broke out above them. The rival suitors screeched and scrambled back and forth from one end of Pat's attic to the other. Pat thought the fight would end momentarily, but the noise and violence of the conflict kept escalating. Suddenly, there was a loud crash in the garage. Pat went running just in time to see two huge raccoons scramble back up the walls and disappear into a gaping hole they had created when they came plummeting through the garage ceiling, bringing about ten square feet of Sheetrock and insulation down with them.

Pat had reached the end of her rope. She called a wildlife removal expert, only to discover there was then a quarantine in effect in Texas that prohibited the transportation of rabies-susceptible species such as raccoons. In effect, the raccoons could not be removed from Pat's property without breaking the law.

Pat and I discussed what to do. She called a raccoon expert, who advised her to scoop up fresh dog poop every morning and distribute it throughout her attic. The expert said raccoons hated dogs and the smell of the poop would discourage them from staying in the attic. Pat told me she could hardly blame them for that, and worried that the smell might be a bit much for her to bear too. Nor did she relish the idea of sneaking out in the early hours to collect fresh dog poop each morning. She wasn't certain what this would do to her reputation with her neighbors. So Pat found herself unable to comply with this advice, and asked what else the expert would recommend.

Pat was next advised to spray her attic with ammonia each evening, once again working on the noxious smell theory. The ammonia did chase off the raccoons, but they always returned as soon as the smell evaporated. They recommended playing loud, obnoxious rock music in the attic, but it did nothing to disturb the raccoons, and kept Pat and her children more awake than ever.

Pat then bought some vinyl-coated steel hardware cloth. The

next time the raccoons exited the attic, she nailed the rigid metal mesh over the hole, sealing it completely. She put a humane trap baited with the raccoons' favorite cat food in the attic in case one or more of the raccoons was still inside the house. That evening, she heard the trap spring shut and discovered she had captured a large raccoon. Because of the rabies quarantine, the wildlife experts told Pat the only thing she could do with the raccoon that was legal was to release it on her property, so the next morning, Pat let the raccoon loose in her backyard and he hightailed it for the nearest tree.

A couple of peaceful months went by, then Pat once again heard scratching in the ceiling of her bedroom, near where the original entrance hole had been. When she investigated the next morning, she saw that the steel reinforced hardware cloth had been bent back like it was a piece of cardboard. The raccoons were back.

I connected to them through Pat's energy and found just the one female I had communicated with originally. She told me she was pregnant and her babies were due any day. She needed some place to raise her litter. Pat is too kindhearted for her own good sometimes, so she agreed to let the raccoon mother stay if she would be quiet. There were not too many other options available to her because of the rabies situation.

Another couple of peaceful months went by, then the babies left the nest and started wrestling and chasing each other all over the attic. Since they were infants, they were not very responsive to my requests that they behave themselves.

Pat and I were still trying to figure out what to do when her house became quite hot. Pat called a contractor who discovered that the raccoons, to relieve their own discomfort from the Texas heat, had sliced open the air-conditioning ducts in Pat's attic, and were living in cool comfort above while she and her children sweltered below. Both Pat and I were incredulous, but the contractor insisted that raccoons frequently "air-conditioned" attics to maintain their own summertime comfort. He said he had seen many such examples of raccoon intelligence and inventiveness in the course of his work.

Pat had another shock when she finally called her insurance company. The raccoons had caused more than five thousand dollars in damage during their nine-month stay, but the actuary assured Pat her case was not unusual. She said raccoon damage was the number one cause of homeowner claims in our area.

Pat rented the humane trap again, unhappy that such traps, while securing the animal without injury, can hold just one animal at a time. She knew there was a family in her attic, but hoped that if she released them all in the same area, they could find each other again. Then Pat and her family could finally have some peace of mind, and a house free of ongoing damage and constant, all-night noise from the raccoons.

Over the course of the next three weeks, Pat trapped the adult female and two of her babies, old enough at that point to be called juveniles. After checking to make sure the raccoon mother was no longer nursing, Pat released her in a park close to a lake, which she hoped would ensure an abundant source of food and water. Pat told me the mother sang a woeful, trilling song when she was released, a noise unlike anything Pat had ever heard from a raccoon's throat. I knew the raccoon was heartbroken because she was being taken from her babies, but she was no more heartbroken than Pat, who was suffering agonies of guilt over the entire situation.

As I mentioned earlier, Pat had planned to release the babies in the same spot as the mother, with the hope they could reunite their family in the wild. But it was several days before the first juvenile went into the trap. In the interim, we had a heavy rain which washed away all traces of the adult female's scent, so the babies wouldn't have been able to track their way back to their mother.

After she trapped the first juvenile, Pat sought the advice of the Texas Wildlife Center, who told her that releasing such a young animal in the wild, even in the same area in which its mother had just been released, would be an almost certain death sentence. Raccoons stay with their mother for at least a year while she teaches them to hunt and protect themselves from their natural predators such as owls, hawks, dogs, and humans. These babies were old enough to provide themselves with an adequate, if somewhat limited, diet, but their mother had not yet taught them all the lessons they needed to learn in order to survive and live a normal life in the wild.

In addition to rabies, there was an epidemic of distemper among raccoons in our area, and the experts, though legally unable to ask Pat to bring the juvenile to them, strongly suggested they would know best how to deal with it. So Pat took the darling little animal, knowing full well she was breaking the law, but not having any other choice. She had to get the raccoons out of her attic as quickly as possible so she could have repairs made and secure her home once again.

The people at the center are dedicated to wildlife, and hold the interests of wild animals over those of humans, as well they should. They told Pat that raccoon habitats are rapidly being destroyed by urban sprawl and overbuilding, and the animals have no choice but to invade homes during cold winter months so they can survive and stay warm. Pat felt very sad that the raccoons' natural habitat had collapsed, but knew she could no longer share her attic with them.

There are several remarkable things about this story. One is the responsiveness of the adult female raccoon to telepathic communication. Every time we asked her to quiet down, she did so immediately. And yet the adult males, in the throes of springtime passion, ignored our pleas for consideration. The babies too were difficult to instruct, because they were so little and playful.

Pat believes, as I do, that we all have a responsibility to care and provide for animals; that they have as much right to be here as we humans do. She knew raccoon habitats were being destroyed, but did not know why they were invading so many homes in our area, which is heavily forested. Pat thought there should have been plenty of potential raccoon homes available in the many large trees growing all around us.

Pat started investigating and discovered the reason the raccoons had chosen her home instead of one of the dozens of mature trees in her backyard is that raccoons cannot live out in the open. They must have a protected shelter in which to sleep, winter over, and raise babies. This information got Pat to thinking . . . if raccoon damage was the number one cause of homeowner insurance claims in our area, then raccoons must be responsible for damaging homes in other areas also.

Pat came up with the idea of developing an artificial "coon hollow" which homeowners could attach in a tree in their backyard to attract raccoons. Admittedly, it would not be heated or air-conditioned, but if properly designed, it could prevent problems for many homeowners while providing raccoons with a suitable place to live. Once Pat has a prototype of her coon hollow available for testing, I'm sure we will have many more "raccoon stories" to share.

I am sure there are people out there who think Pat went a bit overboard, whose first response to the raccoon invasion would have been to get out the poison or shotgun. To these people I say, every animal was put here by God for a reason. They all play a vital role in the ecological balance of our earth and when we start trying to play God, without regard for the innate balance that exists in all of nature, we get into real trouble.

History is full of stories of ecological disasters that have occurred after man recklessly altered the balance of nature to satisfy his own needs of the moment. Before you decide to eliminate a raccoon, consider that they kill and eat poisonous snakes, yellowjackets, grubs, larvae of many insects destructive to our crops and ornamental shrubbery, slugs, carpenter and fire ants, carpenter bees, and many types of destructive beetles. Yes, raccoons, birds, and other wild animals may occasionally spoil some of your garden vegetables, but just remember the old and wise poem:

> One for the birds
> One for the bees
> One for the Good Lord
> And one for me.

I've never known a person who could eat all the production from their gardens, so why not share your abundant harvest with wild animals? Humans do not hold an exclusive right to exploit the earth's bounty for their needs alone. The fruits of the earth were put here for animals to enjoy too.

Man is destroying wildlife habitat at a terrifying rate. Where are wild creatures supposed to live if we bulldoze all their trees and hollows? What are they supposed to eat? It is incredible so many wild animals have adapted and learned to live close to us. If we don't make accommodations for the animal kingdom in our planning, then we are dooming ourselves to future problems, and perhaps, even signing the planet's death certificate. Maintaining a proper ecological balance and learning to coexist in peaceful abundance with all the earth's creatures are absolutely essential if the human race is to survive.

Repairs to Pat's home were scheduled, but the story hadn't ended. Pat was very concerned about the two juveniles remaining in her attic. The second one she had taken to the Wildlife Center had tested positive for distemper. I connected with the babies and sent them a picture of walking into the trap side by side. I told them that if they did that, they could stay together in a lovely house Pat was having built in her backyard.

The next morning, Pat called me very excited. The two babies were in the trap! The carpenter rushed to complete the raccoon house, then Pat painted it and moved the babies into their new home.

Now, every night around nine-thirty, the raccoons come out on their raised porch to eat and drink, then they are off to explore the neighborhood. But their habitat no longer includes Pat's home, because she has a solid new roof. Acting on the advice of Mona Miller, who has cared for injured and orphaned raccoons for many years, Pat also sprayed a mixture of dog and human hair throughout her attic. In the unlikely event the raccoons break in once again, the scent of the hair will chase them away with its danger signal, and keep them from settling in.

Rutger Hauer

Pat has been so taken up with her raccoon experiences and her decision to try and develop a coon hollow that she tells her story frequently. A friend of hers, Stephanie, had been having difficulty with an aggressive hummingbird who was trying to control access to all seven hummingbird feeders in her back garden. She nicknamed him Rutger Hauer after the famous actor who was most often cast in the role of a tough criminal. Every time another hummingbird approached any of the feeders, Rutger attacked the bird and chased it off.

After Stephanie heard Pat's story, she decided to have a little talk with Rutger. This is an example of what I mean when I say that anyone can communicate with animals. Stephanie had no formal training in animal communication, but she believed she could do it, so she did.

Remember earlier how I emphasized that you must praise an animal to gain its trust and attention? Stephanie started her conversation with Rutger by telling him she realized that he was a "macho, dominant kind of guy bird," and as such, his job was to protect the weaker birds, not attack them. She sent the feisty little bird a picture of the hummingbird feeders and told him to pick one feeder to guard, and let the other hummingbirds share the remaining six. She was picturing this as well as saying it, and sending out the feelings of pride the little bird must have felt at being the "cock 'o the walk."

This must have made sense to the bird, because to Stephanie's amazement, Rutger complied with her request. She suddenly found she could communicate with the birds. She was so pleased and surprised at how simple it really was.

Things were peaceful in Stephanie's garden for a few weeks, then a new challenge was mounted by a bird Stephanie called Sly Stallone. Feeling very confident, Stephanie had the same talk with Sly, sending out the pictures and emotions to match her words, and she experienced the same positive results. He picked another feeder to guard, leaving Rutger and the other birds alone.

Finally, an unusually dominant female showed up. Stephanie dubbed her Elizabeth Taylor, and gave her the talk, and Liz picked a third feeder to guard. Things are currently peaceful, but Stephanie has decided if any more dominant birds show up, she's going to have to start buying nectar feeders wholesale.

Zula

One of my clients, Paula, a great animal lover, was living on a ranch on Galveston Island, where she was feeding and caring for a number of domestic, wild, and feral animals. At the time she called, Paula was in the process of training a possum named Sowelu, whose mother had been killed. When the training was complete, Paula was to release Sowelu in the wild. But the raccoons on the ranch were so fierce that Paula found she couldn't release Sowelu and the possum ended up living in the house like a cat.

Though Paula was calling about her missing cat, Zula, I connected first to Sowelu who was quite chatty. She told me that one night when she walked about the floor one of the cats had scratched her on the nose. Paula confirmed this had happened. Sowelu then told me she was confused about where Paula wanted her to go to the bathroom. When I asked Paula, she said she wanted the possum to use the litter box just like the cats. Paula said from that time forward, the possum never missed the litter box again. Then Sowelu complained that Paula had cleaned the floor under her bed with something that smelled horrible. When I asked Paula, she laughed and said she had been using a pine-scented cleanser, another example of how something chemical, which may smell quite pleasant to humans, can upset the sensitive noses of our animal friends, who like natural and not artificial odors.

There was a strong strain of Maine Coon Cat running among the feral cats on the ranch. Paula had adopted two females, Sylphan and Keffie, and a male she named Zula, a magnificent specimen of Mackerel Coon Cat, who had an apricot underbelly to set off his distinctive raccoon-like markings. Though still somewhat feral, Zula had become a delightful companion for Paula, always clowning and making funny faces and lying about the house in a variety of unusual positions. It especially amused Paula when Zula fell asleep on his back with all four paws in the air. His sudden disappearance broke Paula's heart.

Sylphan came through next and informed me she was a very smart cat who had an exceptionally beautiful tail, and confessed it was she who had scratched Sowelu. Then she told me Keffie had a terrible pain in her back and could hardly walk. Paula confirmed this too and told me Keffie had been quite ill with a variety of complaints for some time.

I connected with Keffie and told Paula she had a pinched nerve in her back, which could be helped with absent healing. I sent healing energy to Keffie and knew that my guides had relieved her pain.

But now my worry was Zula. Paula had searched the ranch with no luck. I quieted myself and suddenly connected with a cat who told me he had once fallen into the water and had to swim very hard to keep from drowning. When I told Paula she became very excited and said, "We've got him!" because Zula, who was given to parading up and down railings, had once fallen from a rail into the canal which ran near the ranch house. We knew then that he was alive.

I asked Zula what had happened that caused him to leave the ranch. He said he had been fighting off the raccoons by standing on the back deck and hitting them on the head. Then two of the raccoons charged the deck and he ran through the sliding glass door into the house, with the raccoons in hot pursuit. He told me the raccoons were really mad by then and he was afraid of their wrath. Raccoons have very sharp claws and teeth, which they won't hesitate to use in a fight, so Zula was right to be concerned about his safety, especially as he had been aggravating the raccoons.

Paula told me Zula knew to let the raccoons alone and was surprised to hear he had been teasing them. She provided plenty of food for both her cats and the raccoons so it shouldn't have been an issue of fighting over the food. But Zula told me he had told the raccoons to clear off because this was his house and his territory, and he didn't like sharing it with them.

Zula told me the raccoons chased him through Paula's kitchen, out the cat door and down the front deck stairs. They kept right on chasing him, and he was frightened so he hadn't stopped running until he was off the ranch. I asked Zula which way he went and he sent me a picture of turning left as he went away from the ranch. That made sense to Paula who told me there was only one way to leave the ranch; you couldn't go north because of the water, and the road went south. That was where Zula had gone.

I asked Zula for any unusual landmarks he might have seen along the way and he transmitted a picture of several houses. The most distinctive one was a large house with a lighted tower that looked like a steeple. Paula knew exactly where this house was. Zula said he went past there and then went through a field. Though I had never been to Galveston Island and was miles away at my office during these communications, Paula said the physical descriptions I was giving her were very accurate. She said the field Zula mentioned led to a couple of developments; one called Kahala Beach and the other called Indian Beach. Paula already had prepared flyers. Using the information I had received from Zula, Paula went to those locations and put her flyers out. She spoke to everyone she saw about her beloved cat.

Though Zula loved Paula, he was jealous of the attention she paid the raccoons and a bit afraid they would hurt him if he returned to the ranch. He liked it where he was, and planned on staying. I asked him for some more landmarks and he sent me a picture of a satellite dish. This was most helpful to Paula, who told me that such dishes were forbidden by deed restrictions in Kahala Beach, but not in Indian Beach. We were gradually narrowing down the field of search.

The next day, two workmen called from Indian Beach and told Paula they had seen Zula. She called me again and when I connected to Zula, he told me he had seen the men and that their truck was dark blue, which Paula said it was. She started leaving food for Zula on the beach at that location, and quickly discovered there was a large colony of feral cats living there. Paula started staying out late at night, sitting on a beach chair on Indian Beach, hoping for some glimpse of her pet. Though she saw many cats, there was no sign of Zula.

The following week, Paula called to consult me again, distraught that she hadn't seen Zula. She wanted me to tell her once more about the landmarks. I described the scenery leaving the ranch for her, including an old house on the land and another outbuilding.

Then Zula sent me a picture of a brown tabby he really liked, liked so well in fact that he had taken her on as a mate. There were two kittens with her, a white and gray, and a calico. He sent me a picture of the drainage culvert where he found them looking for water. The mother cat and her babies were all feral.

When I told this to Paula, she thought I was way off base because Zula had been neutered. I told her it was still possible for Zula to desire the company of a female cat despite his operation, but she thought I was wrong about the mother cat and her kittens.

That evening Paula went to the beach to put out food. She lay in the beach chair for a couple of hours, reading by flashlight and waiting for Zula to appear. Suddenly Paula felt intense energy at her shoulder. She turned and there was the brown tabby mother cat lying about one hundred yards off in the field with her two kittens, one calico and the other gray and white, just as Zula had said. From that time forward, the tabby let Paula see her all the time, but there was still no sign of Zula.

Then just as suddenly, the mother cat stopped appearing. I told Paula that Zula had told the tabby to stop coming out to her. By this time, Paula was emotionally drained, and she questioned whether we really were in touch with Zula or not. I could see the pain and frustration in her face. I asked Zula to tell me something only Paula would know, and he confessed he used to relieve himself in the water bowl to keep the dogs and raccoons away. When I relayed this to Paula, she was elated, because Zula had done that. But she still wondered why he would never show himself to her. He told me he was afraid Paula would take him back to the ranch where the wild raccoons were, and he was very happy where he was and did not want to be removed. That was why he told the mother cat to quit going out when Paula visited.

Paula's friend Annette did see Zula at night on more than one occasion, but Paula never did. He would tell me what Paula was wearing when she came to the beach, so we knew he was watching her. I felt this was the oddest situation. Here was a cat who obviously loved his mistress, and she was crazy about him and mourned his absence to the point where she sat on a deserted beach every night hoping to see him. Yet he would not show himself. He told me what she wore, where she sat, who she talked to and what she said, but he could not be convinced to come out.

Paula reluctantly accepted the fact that the beautiful cat she had rescued from a feral life had freely chosen to return to that precarious existence. She still put out food, but the hope that she would get her pet back began to fade.

Then something changed. Paula moved to Houston, and was unable to go every night to put out food and water. We were in the middle of a fierce drought. When last I connected with Zula, he complained about Paula's absence and of being thirsty and hungry. I told him that Paula had moved far away, and encouraged him to end his standoff and come forward. I told him he could bring his companion and her offspring, and they would have all the food and water they wanted, whenever they wanted. Zula said he would think about it, but emphasized he had to be free. He had lived as a feral cat before, and his freedom was the most important thing to him. He loved Paula very much but did not want to be shut in a house.

We are still in touch with Zula. Fortunately, the drought ended with the onset of the tropical storm season, so Zula and his family are no longer thirsty. But they still live a very dangerous and uncertain life. Paula is planning to move back to Galveston soon, and it is my feeling that when she moves into her new house, Zula will return to her, secure in the knowledge that he will not have to deal with the raccoons anymore, and his desire for freedom will be respected.

THESE stories show how telepathic communication can be used to establish a link with either wild or feral animals. You do not have to have any special training, just an open mind. Anyone can use the techniques outlined in chapter 12 to establish better communication with animals, whether wild or domestic.

Once you have learned to establish this special bond, the

hardest thing is learning how to let go. But there comes a time when every animal dies. That is what I discuss in the next chapter, how to cope when a beloved pet passes on to the next dimension.

CHAPTER FOURTEEN

Fond Farewells

How to Cope When a Beloved Pet Dies

*P*erhaps the most difficult time I ever lived through was the illness and death of my beloved Rhodesian Ridgeback, Bella. I had her from a small puppy, and over the years, she had become my most constant companion.

For each of us who share our lives with pets, the time comes when we must say goodbye. No one likes to think about their beloved pet dying, but since few animals other than parrots and tortoises have a life span comparable to that of humans, the day of grief is inevitable.

Domestic dogs and cats live an average of just ten to fifteen years, so during the course of our lives we may have to say goodbye over and again, first to one beloved animal companion, then to another. I know from experience the pain does not lessen with repetition. Each time we lose a pet, we feel the sadness intensely.

But we must let our animal companions go when their time comes. The greatest gift we can give a dying pet is to send them on their way with our love and blessing so that they may make the transition from this earth plane to the spirit world with dignity and at peace. If our grief at the thought of their death and our fear of what life will be like without them are so unmanageable that we cannot let our pets go, we cause animals that are in horrible pain to hang on and on, just to please us. That is a terribly irresponsible and unfeeling thing to do.

While I am speaking of responsibility, I want to remind you to be sure and make arrangements for your pet's ongoing care in case you yourself should precede your animal companion in death. I know of many pets that have been tossed out on the street by unfeeling relatives, or taken to shelters to be killed after their loving owner passes on, simply because their human companion failed to plan for their future needs. You must specify exactly how you want your pet to be cared for, and by whom. If you are able to leave a bequest to cover your animal companion's needs after your passing, so much the better.

If you can, make arrangements for a reliable friend with whom your pet already has a loving and familiar relationship. Ask if they will take your pet in the event of your death. This will allow you to feel comfortable about your animal companion's future if you pass on before they do. If your finances permit, leave money adequate to provide for your pet's care and outline your wishes for that care precisely in your will, including the name of the person who has agreed to care for the animal. Do this even if you are young and in the prime of health, because none of us knows with any certainty the exact day and method of our own passing. If you walk out the door and get hit by a car today, your beloved pet could be hungrily wandering the streets or sitting in a cage at the pound tomorrow.

Death is a natural part of life, but sometimes we humans lose track of that reality. In our imaginations, we paint death in dark and frightening tones. But we must remember that animals do not share our human fear of death; what they do fear is causing their human companions pain when they depart their physical bodies and pass over to the spirit world. That is why they will struggle to hide an illness or injury, to save us from worry, and why a dog or cat approaching the end of its life will often take itself off into the woods to die in private. They choose to go back into the comforting embrace of nature to transition, to spare their humans the agony of watching their passing or of discovering the physical body they've left behind when they passed into spirit.

We attach so much importance to our animal companion's physical bodies. Their soft fur and warmth comfort us, the bright sparkle in their eyes fill us with joy. The sheer exuberance of their delightful and distinctive personalities brings so much love and happiness into our lives that when they do leave we often cannot imagine how we are going to go on without them.

Perhaps it would be helpful and ease your grief if I told you a little about where animals go when they die. Despite what some people are taught—that only humans have immortal souls— I know that animals are spiritual beings. When they die, they do not go off into a void, into dark nothingness. They go to a place of unearthly beauty, where joy, peace, and happiness reign supreme; where memories of pain, care and worries fade into bliss. Knowing this and being the gift of being able to see into the spiritual realm helped me cope when Bella passed over.

When I realized Bella was becoming ill, I connected to her energy and got a feeling of pain in one of my legs. I sensed she had a tumor, and our vet confirmed this. Though I wanted to believe this would be one of my miracle stories, deep inside I knew Bella was very close to leaving her physical form.

For weeks after I learned of Bella's illness, I gave her healing, relieving the pain in her leg and praying that what I knew to be true would not actually turn out to be true. I found it very painful to let her go, hoping that she would just leave her physical form to save me from having to make the decision to humanely end her life to spare her suffering.

Finally, Bella's suffering became too much for me to bear. I asked her if she wanted to go. Though she did not want to leave her family, she said she was ready.

Fitz and Emma and I were heartbroken. I phoned my sons in England, Sean and Patrick, to let them know that Bella's time for leaving us was close. I didn't want my Bella to experience the upset of going to the animal hospital, which she didn't like, so I asked the vet to come to the house so we could all be with her. That way, Bella would be in her home surrounded by her loving family when she left her physical body.

Though I felt tremendous sadness, I knew that when Bella left the earth she would go to a beautiful dimension where she would be happy and free from pain. I told Bella what was going to happen. I told her we would see each other again. I asked her if she would help me in my work with the animals when she passed over. She said she would. (And she does. I see her often and feel her presence while I am working.)

The final evening came much too quickly. We all sat together on the floor with Bella: my husband, Fitz, and I, my daughter, Emma, our cat, Wellington, and Foxy too. I held her beautiful head in my lap, and we gave her permission to leave, to go with our love and blessing. The vet administered a shot that caused Bella to go to sleep as I held her in my arms. I knew the exact moment when she left her physical body. After she passed from her physical body, she thanked me for making the decision to help her go and told me she was happy to get out of her body and away from the pain. She said that when the vet administered that shot she could not leave her body soon enough.

Bella's pain was no more; she was at peace. But our human pain had just begun. She had gone on and we had to learn to live without her, but I knew that her energy would be with me forever. We would never get over the loss; we would just get used to living without her.

That is what I am still doing now—learning to live without Bella's physical presence. I miss her companionship, her compassion, the joy we shared at happy times together, her unfailing love and compassion she gave me during sad times. I miss the feel of her soft velvet coat, the lick of her tongue against my cheek or hand, the beauty and love shining from her eyes for all of us to see, her joyous bark, her paw that lifted each time she wanted attention, the comfort of her presence at night on the end of my bed, and the protection that she gave to me at all times. I miss my Bella.

I would like to share with you the poem my son, Patrick, sent to me from England after Bella passed over. It has comforted me greatly.

Bella's Eulogy
by
Patrick James

When we lose a friend like Bella,
only passing time can make a difference
to the way that we all feel.

And when her loss hurts really hard,
by looking back and remembering, we can find the pleasure
that will help ease the pain and change our tears to laughter
and joy.

> *Bella was a friend like no other, and her loyalty had no*
>   *barriers.*
> *The loving light in all our hearts is Bella*
> *who is within each of us.*
>
> *The love she had for our family was her life,*
> *and our love for Bella was our greatest pleasure.*

Though no animal can take the place of a pet that has passed on, very often the addition of a new pet to the household can ease your loss. In the course of my rescue work soon after Bella's death, my dog Honey came into our lives. I feel as if Bella sent her to us, so that she could look after us and we after her.

Often it does help tremendously if you adopt another animal. You may feel guilty about bringing another animal into your home; that is natural. But don't let your grief keep your home empty of an animal companion for too long. Shelters are full of orphaned animals desperate for loving homes. Remember, you are not trying to replace the animal you have lost; just looking for another animal you can love as much, but in a different way.

It may help you to know that your animal companion who has passed over is hoping that you do get another pet. They want us to have the benefits of companionship with animals and do not feel the senseless jealousy that we humans sometimes fall prey to. If that is a worry that you have, let go of it and make a place in your life for a new animal companion.

Some of you will be unable to adopt a new animal quickly as your grief prevents you from being able to open your heart to a new love. But I can honestly say from experience that getting a new companion animal as soon as feasible after the death of your beloved pet is the best way I know of healing your grief. Many people feel guilty about adding another addition after their friend has gone home to the other side. However, when I talk to the animals that have crossed over, their wish is always that their human companions share their lives with another special animal friend. I still miss Bella and think of her each day, but the presence of Foxy and Honey was a great comfort to me during my initial period of mourning.

Since Bella's death we have lost two more beloved pets, my wonderful cat, Wellington, and a lovely cat Fitz found and brought home. We named her Rosie. Each time, we have felt an intense sense of loss, but have found a way to heal with the love of our other animal companions. We always remember the pets that have passed on with great love and fondness, but we don't let the sadness we feel at their passing keep us from enjoying the companionship of our other animal friends.

Saying goodbye is always very painful, but if your pet is suffering, it is time to let go. If you can understand there is no death and that your pet is going to a wonderful place and will no longer suffer any pain, perhaps you can be happy for him or her. I know you will miss the comfort of their physical presence and the energy of their personality. The house will feel empty and lonely. But understand that they have not left us; they are still with us and they visit us in their energy bodies. We can no longer see them with our eyes or hear their meows or barks with our ears, but we can still feel them in our hearts. We feel and sense their presence in our lives. It is just different because we are still in our physical bodies and they are in their energy bodies. But life does go on.

Don't hold on to your pet for selfish reasons or because you are unable to face the reality of its passing. Remember your pet does not fear death. When animals are ready they welcome the transition from this earth place to a better place. They are not just a physical body any more than we are. Like us, they have chosen to come to this dimension to learn and they have their work to do, but unlike us, they are often glad to leave it, particularly if their physical body has broken down. Still, an animal will hang on to life even though his body is wracked with pain if it knows that its human does not want it to pass over. When your pet is very ill, it is a true act of unselfish love for you to tell him it is okay to pass over and go. You will be doing your pet a great kindness if you can find the courage to do this.

If you are having trouble gathering your strength, try putting yourself in your pet's body. Feel his physical pain and try to understand how it would feel if it were you in that body. Perhaps this will help you make the right decision in a timely and compassionate manner.

Sometimes it is all too easy to overlook your pet's needs. You leave the house and go to work daily, then to the cinema or a restaurant in the evening. You exercise at a gym and continue with the enjoyable activities of your daily life. We are busy and occupied and time passes quickly. But left alone at home, your sick pet no longer can play ball. He is no longer able to go for his walks. He can't enjoy his food. Time goes slowly for him as time does when we ourselves are unhappy and in pain. If you are allowing your pet to live in pain and suffering, ask yourself why. Is it for the few hours or few minutes a day you spend with him? The rest of the time you are off pursuing your activities, with your body fit and well and your mind occupied. Just remember, while you are gone, your pet is suffering alone. His days are long and filled with pain and loneliness.

Remember you are allowing this to happen to him. This is not the way to love your pet, in fact, it is unconscionable. He may be suffering and in pain twenty-four hours a day and you are keeping him alive and in misery for your own pleasure or because of your own imaginary fears. Do him a great kindness and let him go.

I had one client who brought me her very old cat, who was almost twenty and suffering from a variety of health problems. When I connected to the cat's energy, I discovered he was terribly eager to pass over, but was just hanging on because his owner was so adamant about not letting him go. The cat was in a great deal of pain, and I sent him some healing to relieve the pain, then decided to speak to his owner. But she had made up her mind the cat was going to stay no matter what. She was consumed by her fear of losing her cat and completely disconnected from the suffering that her selfishness was causing the cat to endure. She did not realize this was what she was doing.

I continued to work with her for a few weeks, doing what I could to help the cat, whose body was almost totally broken down. I felt very sorry for my client because she was not able to see past her own feelings, but I felt even sorrier for her cat whose physical body had failed him completely. He was trying desperately to hang on for his owner's sake, but he was out of his physical body more than he was in. He was ready to go.

Very patiently, I explained to my client that it was time for her pet to pass over to the next dimension, and that she would be doing him a great kindness to let him go. I told her there was no more that I could do for her or for her pet. It was a decision she would have to make. Finally she was able to come to her senses and let her cat go, and no sooner had she told him he could leave than the cat passed over. He left behind great physical suffering and went to the place of carefree happiness he'd been longing for, but he had loved his human companion so very much that he was determined to hang on in the physical body as long as he could, just to keep her company.

You know if your animal is suffering, so always try to put their needs first when you decide whether to let them go or not. Look inside your heart; trust your intuition and your feelings and you will not go wrong.

But there *are* some animals whose time hasn't come yet. There are many pets that veterinarians have recommended for euthanasia that are walking around happy and healthy because their owners believed they could recover and refused to give up. These are usually animals that have suffered some sort of traumatic injury like being hit by a car or attacked by another animal. If you sense that your injured animal has plenty of life left if you can just get him past the immediate crisis, then you must fight for their lives along with them.

Generally speaking, animals who are suffering from degenerative conditions like diabetes or cancer are not good candidates for this sort of miraculous recovery because as their condition advances they just keep getting sicker and weaker. If your pet has a progressive disease and the vet tells you the outlook is not good, you can certainly look into alternative forms of treatment, but you must be especially sensitive to how your pet is feeling and be sure not to hang on too long and cause unnecessary suffering. The kindest thing you can do for an animal that is suffering is to give him permission to leave his physical body.

You are the only one who can make the decision whether or not to let your pet go. You must decide according to the information that is available to you at the time and the best judgment of the vets who are caring for your animal. The very best way to make such a difficult decision is to trust your heart and your intuition, and do whatever they tell you to do. You will have a gut-level feeling in any case, and following that feeling will not steer you wrong.

If you feel your pet's life should be ended, go with that

feeling. Make the decision and stick with it. Do not berate yourself or allow yourself to be eaten up with guilt if you must euthanize an animal.

If you think there is a chance for recovery, go with that. You can always change your mind if your animal's condition deteriorates significantly. The important thing is to not let anyone else make this decision for you.

Of course we all hope our pets will die naturally. But sometimes it is not so easy. We have to take responsibility for our animal friends, and sometimes, when they are lingering in pain, we have to make the heart-wrenching decision to end their lives humanely so that we may also end their suffering.

The question of burial is a matter of individual choice. Some of you will prefer to have your animal buried on your property. Others prefer cremation of their pet's remains so they can carry the ashes with them in case they move.

Sometimes it is helpful to have a small passing over ceremony to help you accept the fact that your pet is really gone. My cat Wellington adored frogs so I have made him a lovely little grave in my garden, adorned with flowers and small statues of frogs. I visit him there every day and it has been a great comfort to me to have a quiet, beautiful place where I can go to visit my beautiful Wellington and he always comes to see me in his spiritual form.

One thing I do recommend is to find a sympathetic vet who will come to your home to put your pet to sleep in its familiar surroundings. If your vet will not do this, keep searching until you find one who will. It really helped me deal with Bella's passing to know that she died in her home, surrounded by the family she loved; the family that loved her in return.

I still see my Bella. Often when I walk Foxy and Honey on the nearby golf course, I can feel Bella's energy and see her running with my dogs. Her spirit is always present around me. I feel it very strongly.

Life is energy. On a spiritual level I know that energy can never be destroyed; it only transforms. Einstein was quoted as saying he believed in an afterlife for this very reason: that energy never dies. So I know that Bella has not truly left us; we just cannot see her physical body except in our mind. But I feel her, I sense and know she is there, still running after the squirrels and the birds, running toward the lake with Foxy and Honey and taking her morning swim.

There are times when Foxy feels Bella's presence too and knows she is with us. I feel my love for her and know that no one can take away what I shared with my special friend: the happiness, the memories, the joy and love. My life and that of all my family has been richer because we were able to share Bella's life.

There came a day when we were able to look forward to sharing our lives with another Ridgeback. One of my clients in Arizona, Anne, called to say she would like to give me a puppy from her next litter. While Bella wanted to come back to me as a Ridgeback puppy, she discovered her true place is working to help me help animals from the other side. Bella is very happy with the work she is doing, helping other animals make the transition from this earth plane to the spiritual realm. So when my new Ridgeback puppy arrived, I sensed immediately that Ellie was a brand-new spirit in my life and that Bella had chosen to stay on the other side and continue her valuable work. Since Ellie's arrival much has happened. We now also have Sabrina, Sammy, Sally and Daisy in addition to Ellie, Honey and Foxy. With the exception of Ellie, all are rescue dogs. I still feel Bella's presence daily and know that one day, when the time is right, she will return to me once again in physical form.

My friend Karen had a little kitten that passed over, and when I asked Bella about it, Bella showed me a lovely picture of herself, swimming across the healing waters that all animals pass through when they pass over, with the tiny kitten resting on her back. As soon as the kitten was no longer frightened, Bella gently rolled it into the water and it swam to the golden shore by itself, where angels were waiting to take the kitten to the spiritual realm.

After animals pass over, they rest for a while, just like humans. Then they have a decision to make, whether or not they want to stay where they are, or reincarnate and go back to the earth in another form to learn more. Occasionally, as Bella has indicated she will ultimately do, they may choose to come back in the same form again, but that is unusual.

I believe humans who are particularly sympathetic to animals have inhabited a variety of animal bodies in their previous lives, so they know the difficulties animals must go through as they make their way in this world, and devote themselves to easing those difficulties whenever they can.

I am unable to tell you how to make your pain go away when your pet is no longer sharing your physical life, or how to cope with your grief. No one else can know how you feel or cry your tears for you. That is an essential part of your recovery, to embrace the feelings of sorrow that you have. It may help to talk to people who understand about the love you had for your animal. The best support you can have is from others who have worked through their own loss. Sadly, many people do not feel about animals as we do, so be sure to find someone who does. Then you can pour your heart out and find some healing, comfort and compassion.

You can't rush through grief. As the weeks pass, you will start to get back into your routine, but follow your own pace. Each of us deals with grief in our own way. Some get on with life quicker than others. I can only tell you to be glad for what you have experienced and learned from sharing your life with your animal companion. Time does help. As I said before, we never entirely get over the loss . . . we just get used to living without our animals that have passed over. The memories are always there and no one can take that away from us; these memories are the jewels in our lives.

When you get to a calmer and less emotional place in your grieving, you will realize that you have experienced a wonderful, close and loving relationship with your animal companion, and a richness and satisfaction you may never experience in a relationship with another human being. The happy relationships we share with our pets are the jewels in our lives. All the material possessions in the world cannot equal this joy. Sharing love with your pet is one of life's sublime experiences. When human beings understand this, the planet will be a wonderful place for us all to live.

Many of you who are reading this book have experienced the loss of a pet. I hope these few words help you turn your sad memories into joyful ones. Remember this is not the end. Know that one day when our time comes to journey home to the next dimension, you will be reunited with your loving friends. When you arrive they will be waiting to greet you. Both of you will be in energy form and will be able to share the same wonderful friendship as you did in physical form.

Epilogue

How You Can Help Animals in Your Everyday Life

Hardly a day passes that I don't see some animal that could benefit from a little human assistance. There are so many unwanted animals, and so many die each year in the shelters because of overpopulation and human neglect.

As much as I love animals, I lived for years in ignorance of the cruelty they were subject to. In fact, when I heard stories of cruelty to animals, I turned away. I didn't want to hear such awful things; they sickened me. My eldest son, Sean James, inherited my love of animals and went to work for the Royal Society for the Protection of Animals, (RSPCA) in London, while still a teenager. Though I was proud of him, I made it clear I didn't want to hear any sad stories, for when I listened, I couldn't get to sleep that night. I couldn't get the horrifying pictures of cruelty out of my mind.

This was during the time I had shut myself off from the world of animal communication, so I was living in a sort of ignorant bliss. I didn't realize how important it was for people who love animals to support animal rights and vigorously oppose the cruel treatment of animals for any reason.

I was working as a fashion model in England, and often had the chance to buy the clothes I modeled at very good prices. I fell in love with a beautiful lynx jacket I modeled at Harvey Nickels, and bought it to wear on a ski trip to the Alps. I wore the jacket for three years in a state of perfect enjoyment, completely unaware of how many animals had sacrificed their lives for this garment.

One afternoon, I was having my tea in our drawing room. I put on the television and sat down to pour. When I looked up, there was a beautiful lynx walking gracefully across the snow. I thought what a magnificent creature he was. Then, to my horror, his leg was caught in a cruel trap which mangled his paw. The pain must have been excruciating. Unable to eat, drink, or move, the lynx was trapped in agony for four days before the hunters returned to check their traps. He began to chew off his own leg in a desperate effort to escape. When the hunter finally approached the lynx, his gun aimed at the cat's head, I could see the relief in the poor animal's eyes. He understood the horrendous torture would soon be over.

The full realization of how many animals had suffered for me to be able to wear my lynx jacket hit me with the force of a thunderbolt. Tears streaming from my face, I took my jacket, walked into my garden, poured lighter fluid on it, and set it on fire. From that day forward, I have never worn another animal pelt on my body.

That event raised my conscience concerning animal welfare, and since then I have worked for the good of animals, a mission that has culminated in the work I am doing today. Now I would like to enlist your help in the fight.

First, you must take responsibility for the animals that are in your care. Treat them with love, kindness and respect, for they are God's creatures and put here for us to care for, not to exploit. Feed them, play with them, and protect them. Have them spayed or neutered to keep from adding to the pet overpopulation problem. Provide proper veterinary care. Give generously of your affection and attention, for animals thrive on this.

Don't crop your dog's tail or ears, or declaw your cat. As I explained in the chapter on responsible pet ownership, these are cruel and unnecessary procedures, relating more to human whim and laziness than any need of the animal. Cats particularly suffer with declawing. It would be like having your fingernails pulled out, one by one. They are left with no way to defend themselves and often resort to biting instead.

If you see an animal being neglected or mistreated, have the courage to do something about it. You do not have to place yourself in danger. Sometimes a phone call to the appropriate agency is enough to rescue an animal in distress. If you can help a neighbor who isn't able to care for a pet but still wants their love and companionship, do so.

Take in lost and stray animals and do your best to reunite them with their owners. Join an animal welfare organization and volunteer your time. Such groups can always use extra help.

Do not support organizations which profit from animal exploitation or cruelty, such as rodeos and circuses. Do not buy products which use cruel and unnecessary animal testing. Don't wear fur. Fake fur today is almost indistinguishable from the real thing, so if you want the look of fur, opt for the fabulous fake instead and save an animal from suffering and dying in some inhumane trap.

If you are taking hormone replacement therapy or HRT, make sure your prescription derives from a plant source. The animal hormone is extracted from the urine of pregnant mares that spend their eleven-month pregnancies standing chained in tiny stalls, without even the room to lie down. Can you imagine never being able to lie down or rest even once during the whole of a pregnancy? As soon as the babies are weaned, they are sold for meat. Then the mares are impregnated and chained up again and again, until they can no longer produce, at which time they follow their babies to the slaughterhouse.

If we all take just a bit of responsibility on our own shoulders, we could do much to reduce the suffering of animals and make this world a better place for humans and animals alike.

Please help.

The Plight of New York City's Carriage Horses

In the course of my work, I often travel to New York City. I like to stay at a hotel that features a spectacular view of Central Park. During my last trip, I felt surrounded by an overwhelming sense of sadness as I stepped from the cab in front of the hotel. I checked in and went up to my room, puzzled by the strong emotions I had felt, and wondered where they had come from. I walked over to the window and threw open the curtains to see the beautiful green park lying before me, but my eyes were drawn by a queue of carriage horses lined up across the street in front of the park. As I looked at them, with their heads down and shoulders sagging with fatigue and resignation, I immediately knew the source of the sadness I had felt a few minutes earlier. It was coming from these poor horses.

Animals have generous and loving spirits and generally speaking, they are happy to help out their human companions in any way they can. The whole notion of domesticating animals came about so that the animal could in fact serve some human purpose, either for companionship or hard work. When we give our animal friends tasks that are beyond their capacities, it is cruel. Animals want to please us; they will try so hard to do what we want that sometimes they place themselves in danger of being injured or overworked.

When we overwork an animal day after day, year in and year out, then they become like these very sad horses. They are without hope of rescue and become resigned to their lives of toil. It is almost as if the light has gone out in their souls, because they do not expect to ever be treated with kindness, love or compassion. As I looked upon the horses standing dejectedly in the street, I felt their sadness and exhaustion. They told me that they worked all day long without stopping, often in bitter cold or extreme heat, pulling carriages with as many as five people plus the driver, sometimes a thousand pounds or more! When you consider that a racehorse may carry no more than a total of 125 to 130 pounds, you will begin to understand how very hard the load is that carriage horses are expected to pull. The vendors feed the horses from buckets and water is available but they do not have the opportunity of grazing on grass. When they finally get home at night, they are wedged into tiny four-by-ten foot stalls, with no room to lie down or even turn around. So after a long day of toil, they are not able to get a proper rest before they have to start out all over again.

After making inquiries, I learned that the stables in New York City that house carriage horses are more than a hundred years old and have no sprinkler system or any other fire safety equipment. In fact, they are little more than crumbling wooden buildings. It surely must be possible to create a situation where both the working and living conditions of these horses can be vastly improved while at the same time allowing the vendors an opportunity to earn a living.

I determined I had to do something to help these horses. The

New York City SPCA sent out enforcement officers who discovered that it was too hot for the horses to work on that sweltering summer afternoon, so they were sent back to the stables until evening came with its cooler temperatures. While I felt good about getting a break for that particular group of horses, I knew that something more had to be done to truly solve the problem for good. I found that the New York chapter of the American Society for the Prevention of Cruelty to Animals (ASPCA) has embarked upon a campaign to get new and more humane regulations passed to govern the carriage horses' working hours and conditions. Current law allows horses to work up to nine hours a day, seven days a week, in temperatures up to ninety degrees Fahrenheit and as low as eighteen degrees Fahrenheit. No provision is made for humidity or wind-chill factors and the effect they might have on the horse's condition, nor are there any requirements about providing regular veterinary care. In short, these animals' lives are miserable. They are forced to pull heavy carriages on concrete streets, bumper-to-bumper around the perimeter of Central Park, breathing in exhaust fumes, with little or no chance to rest during the course of their day. Most of the passengers are unconcerned or unaware about the deplorable conditions under which these horses work. If they were aware, I'm sure people would take a very different view and perhaps even decide against taking a carriage ride to show their sympathy for the horses.

The ASPCA has suggested new laws that would limit horses to working eight hours daily, with a one-hour break near midday. Current law allows a nine-hour workday with no midday break. Minimum stall sizes would be increased to ten-by-ten feet and that would allow a horse to lie down. The current ten-by-four stall size forces a horse to remain standing. The new law also requires fan ventilation, automatic sprinklers and fire extinguishers to be provided in stalls; currently they are not required. Finally, temperature limits would be lowered to eighty-eight degrees Fahrenheit from ninety degrees Fahrenheit and humidity variations would be taken into account to determine if the horses may work or not. Winter temperatures may be no lower than twenty degrees instead of the current eighteen degrees with wind-chill variations taken into consideration to calculate the temperature. Under current law, wind-chill variations are not considered.

These proposed new regulations are definitely a step in the right direction, but I want us to do more. I would like to see the people of the City of New York band together to create a plan that would provide more humane working conditions for carriage horses. If the city built a stable in a corner of Central Park, then all the carriage horses could be housed there and turned out at night to frolic, graze, socialize with other horses and exercise, as horses were meant to do. The individual stalls would be large enough to allow the horse to lie down and rest at night, instead of being forced to sleep standing up as most now do and living under the deplorable conditions that exist today. The carriage routes should be limited to streets within the park, to avoid exposing the horses to excessive traffic, noise and pollution. The city could charge the owners of the horses a fair rent for the stables, thus helping to recoup the cost of building the facility while keeping the carriage business an economically feasible way to make a living. Centralizing the carriage horses into one facility in Central Park would do many things. It would simplify the policing and regulation of the carriage horse trade, it would vastly improve conditions for the carriage horses themselves, and also for the patrons who enjoy carriage rides. Finally, it would eliminate the hazard of having a slow-moving, horse-drawn carriage stuck in a traffic jam in the middle of the city.

If you are a resident of New York City, you can help the ASPCA in their campaign to pass laws providing more humane working conditions for the carriage_horses. Simply visit the ASPCA's web page at *http://www.aspca.org/site/PageServer? pagename=lobby campaigns nyccarriagehorses* and click on the blue "Take Action Now!" button to let Mayor Bloomberg and other top NYC government officials know you support more humane treatment of carriage horses. Together, we can ensure that the carriage horses of New York City have better living conditions and are treated more humanely.